P9-DMZ-569

How Football Explains America

Also by Sal Paolantonio

Frank Rizzo: The Last Big Man in Big-City America

The Paolantonio Report: The Most Overrated and Underrated Players, Teams, Coaches, and Moments in NFL History with Reuben Frank

How Football Explains America

Sal Paolantonio

TRIUMPH
BOOKS

Copyright © 2008 by Sal Paolantonio

No part of this publication may be reproduced, stored in a retrieval system, or transmitted in any form by any means, electronic, mechanical, photocopying, or otherwise, without the prior written permission of the publisher, Triumph Books, 542 South Dearborn Street, Suite 750, Chicago, Illinois 60605.

Triumph Books and colophon are registered trademarks of Random House, Inc.

Library of Congress Cataloging-in-Publication Data

Paolantonio, Sal, 1956–
  How football explains America / Sal Paolantonio.
    p. cm.
  Includes bibliographical references.
  ISBN-13: 978-1-60078-046-2
  ISBN-10: 1-60078-046-6
  1. Football—United States—History. 2. Football—Social aspects—United States—History. I. Title.
  GV954.P34 2008
  796.332—dc22

                                                                      2008019175

This book is available in quantity at special discounts for your group or organization. For further information, contact:

Triumph Books
542 South Dearborn Street
Suite 750
Chicago, Illinois 60605
(312) 939-3330
Fax (312) 663-3557

Printed in U.S.A.
ISBN: 978-1-60078-046-2
Design by Patricia Frey
Photos courtesy of Getty Images unless otherwise indicated.

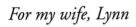

For my wife, Lynn

Contents

"Everybody loves football, don't they?"

—Steve Mariucci, former NFL head coach

Prologue

It was the most-watched sporting event in American television history. And I was missing it.

The New York Giants were cobbling together the most unlikely comeback ever on a pro football field, Eli Manning was about to buy himself a house in Joe Namath's neighborhood, the undefeated New England Patriots were about to cough up a chance at immortality, and I couldn't see it.

It was dusk on February 3, 2008, and all this was taking place under the closed retractable roof of University of Phoenix Stadium in Glendale, Arizona, and across America nearly 100 million people were mesmerized in front of their flat screens, wide screens, and big and small screens, watching Super Bowl XLII. Manning was caught in a three-pronged human vise of Adalius Thomas, Jarvis Green, and Richard Seymour. But, somehow, Manning wriggled free and heaved the football—"a Hail Mary," Rodney Harrison would later call it—toward little-used wide receiver David Tyree, who pinned it between his red-and-white-gloved hand and his royal-blue helmet, and days later appeared on the cover of *Sports*

Illustrated and on a couch next to Jay Leno, explaining to America his improbable journey into a world inhabited by only Boyd Dowler, John Taylor, and Lynn Swann. And even though I was there, as a reporter covering the game for ESPN, I never saw any of that.

The great irony is that while 71,101 disbelieving, delirious fans were inside the stadium, which looks like a cross between one of those bright tin-foil Jiffy Pop containers fully pregnant with popcorn and an odd alien spacecraft that didn't quite make the final cut in *The Empire Strikes Back*, I was stuck in a bewildered and frustrated knot of TV reporters and producers, on a long concrete apron in the unusually damp Arizona evening, waiting for a giant thick steel door—obviously designed with al-Qaeda in mind—to open and let us in for the postgame interviews. We were waiting behind carts and carts of those police barriers that look like bicycle stands and 20-dozen temporary security personnel wearing yellow Windbreakers, waiting to go first—to actually provide a wall of humanity and metal that would prevent us from reaching the triumphant players we were pre-staged to interview.

My colleague, Trey Wingo, had his cell phone pressed up against his left ear. From his home in Denver, another colleague, Mark Schlereth, was providing the game details and—like Ronald Reagan, who used to get the teletype of the baseball games in Chicago and re-create the play-by-play for radio audiences across the Midwest in the 1930s—Wingo barked out each play of the most dramatic fourth quarter in Super Bowl history, and we hung on every detail like the last survivors on a besieged planet.

And I was processing the perfectly symmetrical irony of it all. Here I am, a national correspondent for ESPN, the most-watched sports network in the history of worldwide television, and my job is to observe these events, using every ounce of curiosity in the deep reservoir of my 25 years of reporting experience, and deliver to the viewers a unique observation, an incisive bit of analysis—anything

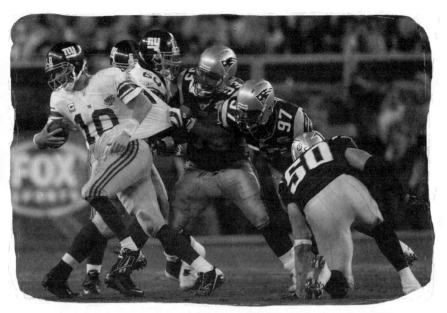

Eli Manning and the Giants provided an improbable ending to Super Bowl XLII.

that would justify the fact that I've been given the honor of getting paid to attend this event.

But in a great twist of fate, in perhaps one of the most important moments in NFL history, I had been stripped of my status as television-content provider. I had been unwittingly jettisoned from that privileged perch and was now a member of the television audience, which in this case turned out to be nearly one-third of all men, women, and children from Cape Cod to California. And it was at that moment that I began to fully understand and appreciate the powerful connection between football and America. Deprived of the opportunity to see and hear and feel the game, I was like some junkie desperate for a fix. I wanted to know what happened, how it played out. Even without the images, I was still addicted to the story itself—maybe even more so. I wanted to know what happened to the hero, Eli Manning, on the final steps of his journey. At that moment, I imagined him as any other fictional protagonist—Odysseus, Indiana Jones, or Luke Skywalker—trying to prevail against forces arrayed by the gods, the unforgiving wilderness, or, in this case, the maniacal genius of Bill Belichick. And what would happen to the Patriots who, in the final acts of the 2007 NFL season, had been portrayed more and more as the villainous occupiers of a land they did not deserve—would they be vanquished in the end?

Standing outside that stadium, I really began to understand how football explains America.

It's funny, too, because everything you read about how football became so popular in America, every scholar you talk to, you come up with the same answer: television made football spectacularly powerful in America. Every conclusion is nearly the same: TV grew up with Unitas and Lombardi and Namath, and that explains how football and America were woven together to become the most profitable professional sports empire known to man.

Well, they have televisions in Japan, don't they? In fact, they have more televisions per capita in Tokyo than they have in New York or Chicago. So, if American football is so perfectly suited to presentation on television, why didn't TV make football popular in Japan? Or England and Germany, or South America and South Africa? They have television in those places. The same color images are parading across the same screen dimensions. How come football is not popular there?

And if it is TV that drives the popularity of American football, then why—after years and years of trying, and millions and millions of dollars invested—has the power of American television (apologies to Beckham and one-fifth of the Spice Girls) failed so spectacularly in making soccer a popular spectator sport in this country?

What is it about American football that resonates here and fails to catch on abroad?

The answer is in the complex fabric of America itself—all starting about the time Colorado joined the union in the year of our nation's 100th birthday, on the muddy Ivy League fields where they played a nasty little game nobody had the patience to watch. It all started when the men playing that game decided on a few simple changes in the rules to Americanize something that had been bequeathed to them by a bunch of wool-clad ruffians from England and Wales. One of those rules changes was clearly inspired by the cultural and economic forces of the nation's march across the continent in the late 19th century, known collectively as Manifest Destiny, a movement that these days is treated with embarrassment and disdain. But, in this book, in explaining *How Football Explains America*, how Europe's games of soccer and rugby evolved into the singularly American game of football, the role of Manifest Destiny will be embraced. So, please, by all means, check your political correctness at the gate. What follows here is an unabashedly celebratory explanation of how in the world we dedicate our Sunday afternoons to the poetically violent rituals of the National Football League. And how in the world I managed to miss the end of Super Bowl XLII.

———

Joan Didion, the great American essayist, wrote at the beginning of *The White Album*, her anthem to the '60s in California, "We tell ourselves stories in order to live. The princess is caged in the consulate. The man with the candy will lead the children into the sea…. We live entirely by the imposition of a narrative line upon disparate images, by the 'ideas' with which we have learned to freeze the shifting phantasmagoria which is our actual experience."

In the late 1890s, deprived of the actual experience, of the actual game, fans of University of Pennsylvania football would gather in front of *The Philadelphia Inquirer*, one of the nation's oldest newspapers, to watch the story of the game recreated minute-by-minute in a storefront window, not unlike the size and shape of what a television would look like decades later.

There was such a demand for Penn's games that the *Inquirer* created a little promotional device called "Miniature Gridiron." Just like Trey Wingo outside University of Phoenix Stadium more than 100 years later, the *Inquirer* editors would take in the teletype dispatches of the game and then update the movement of the players on the field and "freeze the shifting phantasmagoria" to create a narrative, a story that became immensely popular. And sold newspapers. "The invitation to readers to witness these creations at the *Inquirer* building appeared directly under the masthead on the front page," writes Oregon State professor Michael Oriard in his book, *Reading Football.*

As the nation grew more sophisticated and literate, it wanted to celebrate its own story—of cowboys and outlaws and pioneers and gangsters and scoundrels, but also the real-life characters playing the games Americans were now playing themselves. The sports pages were filled with stories of baseball, and of course boxing and horse racing to satiate the appetite for gambling America had inherited from Europe. The Old-World game of football, which was really an amalgam of soccer and rugby, played at Harvard, Yale, Princeton, Penn, and Rutgers, contained none of the compelling, dramatic narrative that translated well into a newspaper story. Go ahead, you try going to a rugby game and writing about it. Soccer? Ninety minutes of whatever, and then maybe one goal scored by accident. Tough to create a coherent narrative out of that.

Remember these three years: 1876, 1880, and 1882. While the years 1958, 1969, and 1993 were pivotal in helping to form our current obsession with the modern game of pro football, it was those dates back when the country was barely 100 years old that really marked the end of a game that had been handed down to America, and the beginning of a game that would become our own.

In 1876, the year of the country's centennial celebration, players from Harvard, Yale, Princeton, and Columbia formed the Intercollegiate Football Association to determine a common set of rules for what was then a game that sometimes looked like soccer and sometimes looked like rugby. That simple meeting more than 130 years ago was inspired by the desire to make the American game more interesting to both players and spectators—something that is still done today. Every year, the NFL holds a spring meeting of its owners, general managers, and coaches, and thinks about how the game can be improved. Something called the Competition Committee—an ad hoc group of coaches and general managers—actually tries to find ways to make the game more competitive and appealing.

It's corporate. It's democratic. It's American. (And it doesn't happen in other sports—not with that kind of regularity.)

It's exactly what happened in 1880. Four years after the formation of the Intercollegiate Football Association, the game's same group of founding fathers met and created its first new rule: "The man who first receives the ball from the snap-back shall be called the quarter-back…" How American: this rule created possession of the ball and thus, territory. But it also foreshadowed something much more important: among the equals on the field, there was now one man who would later become one part gunslinger, one part field general, who would control the action and become the main protagonist in the drama of the game. Without 1880, there is no 1958—no Johnny Unitas directing the game-winning drive against the New York Giants in the NFL Championship Game, no Joe Namath holding court poolside in Miami before shocking the Colts in Super Bowl III 11 years later, no Eli Manning slaying the perfect Patriots in February 2008 in Arizona.

Two years after creating the possession, the representatives from the four Ivy League schools realized that their game lacked one important element that would release them from the shackles of the European version of football. They created the first down—a clearly delineated way to measure the advancement of the ball. The team possessing the ball could advance it, hold the territory, and defend it. Ah, Manifest Destiny! Initially, you were given three downs to go five yards—don't forget, they weren't passing the ball yet. That would take at least another two decades. Still, these changes were profound.

Thus, in the "evolution of American football from English rugby, the distance from 1882 to 1993 is less significant than that from 1876 to 1882," writes Oriard.

The transformation of the game was instantly recognized—by the players, but, more importantly, by reporters writing about it. And this in turn would help create a more dedicated audience. With the advancement of the ball in five-yard increments, or relinquishing the ball quickly to the other team, the game's dramatic action was formed. There was a story, clearly defined and delineated, on a rectangular field, shaped like America.

In 1879, *The New York Times* story about a Yale-Princeton game on Thanksgiving Day was more concerned with what happened in the sparse crowd than the happenings on the field. The subhead read: "Incidents of the Game and Scenes in the Crowd." (A sports editor once told me that if I ever wrote about the crowd at the game, I could buy a ticket and go sit with them.) Then, as now in modern soccer, what was happening in the crowd was often more compelling than what happened on the field.

After the rules modifications of 1880 and 1882, the change in coverage was immediate. "The daily press," writes Oriard, "then taught the public how to interpret the game, how to read it as a cultural text."

That cultural text constantly evolved. Unlike baseball, which marked our history with changes that were subtle and reflected the pastoral nature of the game, football seems to have always been in a constant state of reinventing itself—each reincarnation explaining who we were, who we are, and who we would like to become.

How else do you explain the direct football lineage between General Douglas MacArthur, Vince Lombardi, and Bill Parcells? The link between the trailblazing Jim Thorpe and the artistry of Joe Montana? The common ground between the great symbol of the establishment, Richard Nixon, and the radical journalist who despised him, Hunter S. Thompson? All of them explain how football explains America.

———

This book is not meant to be a fully realized history of football. Plenty of those exist. Instead, this book will attempt to answer a question that I believe has been—up to this point—insufficiently addressed: why does America love football so much?

Actually, the book that was supposed to put it all to rest, tell the whole story with elaborate packaging and the full backing of the NFL itself, was *America's Game: The Epic Story of How Pro Football Captured a Nation* by Michael MacCambridge of *Sports Illustrated*. It was epic, and it told the story of what happened in breathtaking detail. Anybody interested in football must read MacCambridge's book. It's indispensable. But MacCambridge did not fully explain the *how* in his subtitle. There is plenty of who, what, where, and when. This book will attempt to solve the *why* and the *how*—to fill in the blanks.

For example, MacCambridge, as well as many others, wrote about how television catapulted the NFL onto the national landscape in the late 1950s and the 1960s. But what they don't acknowledge is that, decades earlier, the popular press romanticized college football in the way TV did for pro football—and made it wildly popular before Johnny U and Broadway Joe. Harvard, Yale,

Michigan, and California played in packed stadiums from coast to coast. Red Grange never galloped across a TV screen. But he was as big as Babe Ruth. Hollywood made movies about football—John Wayne's first role was not as a cowboy, but as a football player. An entire magazine industry revolved around the game. TV did not make football popular. What I'll prove is that TV used football to help make itself a powerful industry.

When TV arrived, America was already sold on the stories and the characters and the romance of the game. In a country full of commodities, football sold a sensation—a violent confrontation of men fighting over territory. It's a story as old as mankind. It was just put in a game. George Lucas, the creator of *Star Wars*, once said, "I would feel very good if someday they colonize Mars when I'm 93 years old, and the leader of the first colony says: 'I really did it because I was hoping there would be a Wookie up there.'"

It always comes back to the story, the romance, the sensation of following that one character across the plains, across the universe, across the gridiron, to the final destination—all the way fighting the elements, the bad guys, the Mad Stork, Mean Joe Greene, the Purple People Eaters, L.T., the No Name Defense, the Evil Empire, Lord Vader—take your pick. These names might as well be right out of Greek mythology. Why? Because they're right out of America's mythology. The creation of these characters is central to creating the romanticized story line.

In football, it is design and schematics and technique—that's coach-speak, and it's quite necessary. But that stuff is a commodity. You can sell it, and it may take you to Mars. But sometimes, to get there, you may be inspired by or need a Wookie.

Indeed, in all the sociological studies of sports, there is so much made of the role of the Industrial Revolution and militarism to explain the popular phenomenon of American football. But they usually only scratch the surface.

In 2004, Michael Mandelbaum, a professor at Johns Hopkins University, wrote a book called *The Meaning of Sports: Why Americans Watch Baseball, Football and Basketball and What They See When They Do*, and in it he writes, "Seen from a distance, a football play looks like a pre-modern Western battle…. The ways that football teams customarily seek to advance the ball correspond to the familiar battlefield tactics throughout history."

If that's the case, why is this brand of football only played on our continent, and rejected so fervently in, for example, Europe? This so-called pre-modern Western warfare was invented by the hoplite armies of Greece, perfected by Napoleon, and practiced with an unparalleled ferocity by the armies of Germany in two world wars. In all those countries of the Old World and, now, the Third World, soccer is king. And soccer is not a sport that looks at all like "a pre-modern Western battle." In fact, soccer more closely resembles the tactics of the cavalry-based, invade-and-retreat forces of Xerxes, armies of quick-striking mass movement that were eventually defeated by the armies of Western warfare.

Of course, American football is a violent game. Mandelbaum has got that right, and in that regard his work is thought-provoking. But he is among those who oversimplify it. He misses the key nuances of how and why the American game was created. Therefore he doesn't tell the whole story of how football so seamlessly explains America.

It's important to be careful about throwing around words like "warfare," and "going to battle," and "aerial attack" when analyzing football. Indeed, in the course of my daily reporting on the NFL season after season, I'm very conscious of avoiding those terms. Why? Because it disrespects the brave young American men and women who are actually engaged in combat every day in Iraq and Afghanistan, or have put on the uniform and got shot at, or had to shoot somebody. Nobody is using bullets on an American football field.

In order to draw a straight line between military culture and pro football, we will not have to use those terms, as many sociologists have done. That would be the cheap way to illustrate the profound influence that places such as West Point and Annapolis have had on the American game of football.

Many sociologists are also quick to automatically assume that the American game of football was spawned due to the forces of the Industrial Revolution in this country. Mandelbaum, for example, says that American football reflects the industrial age's dependence on measured time and mechanization. "Players," he writes, "are like workers in a factory. They must perform their tasks in a precise sequence…"

There are two problems with that oversimplified explanation of the rise of American football. First: yes, American football is the ultimate team game and often requires the precise movements of each player to succeed. But the game requires, indeed demands, that players have advanced improvisational skill and judgment, at a split second, during which another player may be trying to knock him out or at least use a singularly violent act of collision to prevent him from making a play. Case in point: one of the most celebrated plays in NFL history. It came during the NFL Championship Game on December 31, 1967. Every man and boy in America knows what happened that day in Green Bay. It was the Ice Bowl, Dallas Cowboys against Vince Lombardi's Packers in subzero temperatures. (I watched the game with my father on our Magnavox TV in my boyhood home on Long Island.) Everybody knows how the game was won: Bart Starr, on a quarterback sneak, ducked under the precise block by guard Jerry Kramer of Cowboys defensive lineman Jethro Pugh. Touchdown for Titletown. Packers go on to play in the second Super Bowl. Lombardi gets his name carved on the side of the championship trophy. What everybody doesn't know is that Lombardi, on the sideline, had told Starr to call a fullback plunge. Starr, seeing the ice patches near the goal line, changed the play. That moment of field generalship does not fit neatly into the previously celebrated sociological explanations of how football explains America.

Second point: the last time I looked, the birthplace of the Industrial Revolution was England—not America. The enslavement of the English people to time and factories is a well-established theme in some of the world's great works of fiction. Then, how come they haven't become slavishly attracted to our game of football? What European-based American football team folded more quickly than any other? The London Monarchs. Why? American football was alien to their culture—despite England being one of the world's original industrial societies. Same goes for Germany, which was more highly industrialized, and much earlier than the agrarian-based America of the late 19th and early 20th centuries. Yet, American football was created in a country still very much dominated by the politics and culture of farming, mining, and pioneering. And, in the summer of 2007, the NFL had to pull the plug on the final two teams of the European league of American football. Why? Lack of support. And the experiment with the Tokyo Bowl, an annual preseason game played in Japan, also died due to poor attendance.

In pretty much the rest of the world, soccer is ubiquitous precisely because it is more a reflection of irrational nationalism than a rational, finite adherence to time and precision. That point is brilliantly made in Franklin Foer's terrific bestseller, *How Soccer Explains the World*, which we will address shortly.

To be sure, as science and technology advanced in America, the football fathers were also constantly tinkering with their game, modernizing it, making it more appealing to a changing market and more competitive to players who were growing in skill, smarts, and athletic ability. That's a major theme of this book—showing how other sports stopped evolving and therefore lost their appeal on these shores. Thus, to contend that the American brand of football was just a product of the late–19ᵗʰ century antebellum industrial age is just not enough. If that's the case, then the boys in Manchester would be wearing helmets and picking up the ball with their hands and throwing it 60 yards—instead of just kicking it, like they've been doing for the past 150 years.

Kicking it. That's what the rest of the world does. And that's what I mostly thought about soccer: a game played by a bunch of guys who wish they could pick up the ball and throw it and would like to do whatever it takes to prevent the other guy from doing

Soldiers reenact the raising of the flag at Iwo Jima prior to Super Bowl XLI. Few traditions have become as distinctly American as the game of football.

so, but get red-carded and ultimately removed from the field of competition for trying. No throwing, no blocking, no tackling— and, most important, very, very little scoring. Not American.

But then I read Franklin Foer's book, and I realized I didn't know what soccer was all about. The biggest attraction of the game is not the game itself. It's the fans, the hooligans, and the violent behavior of the game's followers. It's about an unabashed expression of nationalism and—Foer certainly proves—nativism that often jumps off the track of normal social behavior. And, of course, this behavior is often rejected by the country's leaders as barbarian and backward.

Foer quotes one soccer fan in his book with these recollections: "Ten thousand would come to the stadium. Six thousand of them would be up for a fight. The rest came to watch a fight. Yeah, they say they were disgusted. But you'd ask them in a pub afterward, 'Did you watch the fight or the [soccer]?' 'Oh, the fight, of course.'"

Lacking a compelling narrative on the field, soccer fans have to create one off the field—about nationhood, or in the stands—often protecting their turf through alcohol-induced fistfights.

In Britain, where there was enough money to transform the sport, the government was forced to crack down. The last straw came in 1989, when nearly 100 were killed in a mass of humanity pressed against the fences on some terraces that served as a holding pen for fans in Hillsborough Stadium in Sheffield. Stadiums were cleaned up, ticket prices went up, and the game—in some places in the United Kingdom, at least—became somewhat yuppified.

I read Foer's book and thought, well, he has done a brilliant job of explaining how soccer explains the rest of the world. But he's left out a whole universe of people in the United States. Sure, American football has been yuppified, but it didn't happen because Ronald Reagan needed to crack down on fans of the sport. Indeed, if anything, the NFL's transformation to financial superpower took place because the fans were clearly ready to invest millions more in astronomical ticket prices, personal seat licenses, club boxes, sky boxes, and elaborate suites, where they could sip chardonnay and allow the colorful but violent narrative of the game wash over them on Sunday afternoons.

So, deciding that the sincerest form of flattery was a little thievery, I lifted a bit of the title of Foer's book and set out to explain—in a way that we could all understand—how football explains America.

"Simply put, sport is an expression of people's culture," Professor Oriard told me. "Football, the game itself, the narrative on the field, is uniquely an expression of who we are. Football is jammed with underlying mythical structures that we can assign any number of specific themes or narratives."

- Narratives from our Judeo-Christian heritage. The role of religion—from the Catholicism of Vince Lombardi to the Evangelicalism of Tony Dungy—has helped create powerful stories in American football.

- Narratives from our immigrant experience—from the Eastern Europeans and Italian Americans—and from African Americans. All of those ethnic groups forged different narratives within the game of football at different times in our history and helped create the broad appeal that it now commands. On the day after the Chargers beat the Colts in Indianapolis on January 13, 2008, a photograph in the sports section of *USA Today* documented two Colts fans—a boyfriend and girlfriend—consoling each other. The boy's name was identified as Ryan Miller. The name of the girl? Priyn Ishwar. And I said to myself: that says it all about the power of the game to bring people from all walks of life, from every ethnic group, into the big tent of American football.

- Narratives from the still-powerful elements of masculinity and violence in this country. To me the greatest purveyor of those pure motives in the game today is Baltimore Ravens middle linebacker Ray Lewis, who summed it up nicely in *Sports Illustrated* in July 2007: "That's what the game is about. The long runs, the touchdowns and all that, that's the glamour. But the game is about taking a man down, physically and mentally."

- Narratives from our need for the romanticized story line that Americans demand from their television sets every night. It is an undeniable fact that we might as well surrender to: our shared TV experiences—whether it's the O.J. chase, the *Challenger* disaster, the events of 9/11, or just the last episodes of *M*A*S*H* or *Seinfeld*—are some of our most powerful moments as a nation. And what they all have in common is a compelling narrative.

"We tell ourselves other stories in order to live...."

———

Like a good thriller, the story of Super Bowl XLII had a spectacular surprise ending. Baby-faced Eli, the much-maligned kid brother of the celebrated Peyton Manning, led his team down the field, capturing and holding pieces of territory against the evil forces of the Perfect Patriots arrayed against him, and threw a touchdown pass to the often-misunderstood wide receiver Plaxico Burress to capture the first NFL championship for Tom Coughlin, the New York coach finally achieving redemption from his own demons.

After the game, Steve Hirdt, whose job it is to coldly collect somewhat arcane statistics for national television broadcasts, put it best: "It was a morality play."

Yes, Super Bowl XLII was a morality play—and 148.3 million Americans watched at least some part of it. The average audience for the game was 97.5 million Americans—making it the second-most-watched program ever on U.S. television.

I may not have seen the final act, but watching back near my hometown on Long Island was 81-year-old Joseph Patrick Caramente.

When I delivered the *New York Daily News* as a kid, Mr. Caramente was my favorite customer. He wanted the paper delivered very early because he had to drive into the city every morning before dawn to work at Con Edison, New York's power company. In those days—the late 1960s—you could leave your car unlocked in the driveway, and he did. And if the New York Giants or Yankees lost, I was instructed to put the newspaper with the sports headlines on the back cover of the *Daily News* facing down on the front passenger seat of his green Ford LTD sedan. If they had won, back page up.

On the evening of February 3, 2008, Mr. Caramente, who had been suffering through a rare brain disease, was watching his beloved Giants at the Bristal Assisted Living Center in East Meadow, Long Island, with his three best buddies, having the time of his life.

And at that time, the narrative, not the team from New England, was about to achieve perfection. The Giants had a first down on the Patriots' 13-yard line, just 13 yards to go for the game-winning score. Manning, about to reach the journey's end, approached the line of scrimmage and saw the Patriots' veteran linebackers creeping forward, snorting with every step: Junior Seau, playing in his second Super Bowl; Mike Vrabel, playing in his fourth Super Bowl; and the heartbeat of the defense, Tedy Bruschi, playing in his fifth Super Bowl. Manning, playing in his first Super Bowl, saw them coming—all of them. It was an all-out blitz, what the coaches call "zero coverage"—with nobody protecting the back end of the final 13 yards of territory. Here is what the game's founding fathers certainly envisioned 127 years ago—the story line reaching a dramatic climax while the whole world watched.

The ball was snapped to the quarterback. Burress got behind the defense. And Manning released the football. His soft, perfect spiral seemed to take a lifetime to arrive. Burress cradled the ball like it was a child falling from the fifth floor of a burning building. Bruschi dropped to his knees. The Patriots would go home with a single blemish named *Eli* branded on their legacy.

At the Bristal Assisted Living Center on Long Island, Mr. Caramente let out a sigh of joy and relief.

"We were really thrilled he got to watch the end of that game," said his son, Patrick. "And it just made him so happy in the final moments of his life that the Giants won."

The next morning, at about 9:30 on February 4, 2008, Joseph Patrick Caramente of Stewart Manor, Long Island, collapsed from a stroke. He died two days later.

Sal Paolantonio
Moorestown, New Jersey
March 2008

"There was no football, if one may except a New England fashion of kicking a substitute made of a pig's bladder in skylarking fashion after Thanksgiving dinner."

—American football founding father Walter Camp, 1891

How Football Explains
Manifest Destiny

Tedy Bruschi of the New England Patriots walked casually through the tunnel of Giants Stadium, the aging concrete structure in a thousand-acre swamp located about eight miles west of Manhattan, and stepped into the light of an unusually warm Sunday morning on September 9—the first Sunday of the 2007 National Football League season. He stopped. He'd seen this view countless times. This was the beginning of his 12th season. Yet his smile, with the brown-eyed hint of his Italian and Filipino ancestry, had a boyish, naïve glow—for a reason.

He has a hole in his heart. A real hole, not the kind left by an unrequited lover—a hole left by a stroke in February 2005 that would have claimed the professional football career of any normal human being. But doctors performed some kind of newfangled surgery to fix the hole—and, more important, Bruschi is not your normal guy. He has the rare determination of an astronaut, the drive of a stagecoach pioneer. So, even after winning three Super Bowl rings, Bruschi shocked his wife, his coach, and his teammates and came back to play the middle linebacker position with the kind of, well, *heart* few players possess. When he looked up at the sky that morning, he was thinking, *I'm still here. Still doing this.* And he was determined to win one more championship, hoist that trophy named after the guy named Lombardi, who grew up not far from this stadium in northern New Jersey, but was denied a chance to coach his hometown New York Giants and instead went into exile in the small town of Green Bay, Wisconsin, with his unhappy wife, Marie, in 1959, and went on to win five NFL championships, including the first two Super Bowls. That's why it's called the Vince Lombardi Trophy.

It was all there for Bruschi to feel on that Sunday morning—the layer upon layer of story lines filled with ethnic heritage, American history, and current football rivalries, pitting former friends and colleagues against each other in a game and a season that would tell us about ourselves in many more ways than were apparent that day.

The story of Bruschi's cool, aloof, single-minded coach, Bill Belichick, facing off against his former protégé, Eric Mangini, a disciple who strayed to New York to become the head coach of the New York Jets, and who was called "Mangenius" for his stunning one-year turnaround that defied his old boss and landed the freshman coach and his young team in the playoffs a year earlier.

The story of Bruschi's new teammate, the mercurial Randy Moss, who was salvaged from the wreckage of pro football in Oakland, where for two years he wore a Raiders uniform, which Brady never fully embraced. Moss's singularly incandescent talents were now expected to transform quarterback Tom Brady from just your average three-time Super Bowl champion into the kind of player Brady idolized as a child growing up in northern California—that being Joe Montana, the coolest of the cool champion quarterbacks who waved his light saber through the 1980s in a dazzling display of magical championships.

The story of Bruschi's fellow aging comrades on defense— 38-year-old linebacker Junior Seau, who had been voted to the

NFL All-Pro team 12 straight times, but never hoisted Lombardi; 35-year-old safety Rodney Harrison, who had defied age and injury to win two Super Bowl championships with Bruschi; and the gruff ageless linebacker, Mike Vrabel, who had won three Super Bowl titles with Bruschi with a guile and toughness that seem to contradict the fact that he was a pre-med major at Ohio State. Did any of them, on this day, think they had enough left in their legs, and in their will, to make it through a 16-game season, and the playoffs, to win another championship?

That story was week to week, game by game, yard by yard on a field they had to defend inch by inch, beginning with this game filled with hope and redemption, revenge and retribution—a game that would end with a shocking footnote, sending the season and this band of Patriot brothers on a complex, historic journey through one football season that would explain what America is all about.

—————

Long before all this, there was rugby. And it was boring.

Here was this primitive Old World game, brought over from England and played mostly by college boys at Harvard, Princeton, and Rutgers.

And here was a restless nation in the year 1876, the year of the Centennial, when the thirst for new territory, for westward expansion, seemed unquenchable.

So, it didn't fit. Football, as it was being played by European rules in the New World, wasn't an attractive game. The rules of the London Football Association called for players from both teams to mass about the ball, all trying to kick it out to a teammate. In essence, soccer—with a scrum.

"The rules," wrote Walter Camp, the founding football father from Yale, in his landmark book *American Football*, first published in 1891, "forbade any one's picking up, carrying, or throwing the ball in any part of the field. There were no 'off' or 'on' side rules, and the goals were made by sending the ball under the cross-bar instead of over it. Fouls were penalized by making the player who had committed the foul toss the ball straight up in the air from the place where the foul occurred, and it was unfair to touch the ball until it struck the ground."

Under these rules—this is hardly what we now call football—Princeton and Rutgers played a game in 1869, a contest that has often been called the first intercollegiate American football game.

But this Old World game—a blend of soccer and rugby—had no compelling action or story line. It was just a mass of humanity moving in what was then called a "scrummage." Not enough happened. There was no premium placed on advancing the ball, capturing territory, quickly defeating your opponent—the core of what America was becoming. And the players and, most important, the spectators quickly grew tired of it.

The boys at Harvard made the first move. They called it "the Boston Game," which allowed running with the football and tackling. Their game was a little more open and much more physical brand of rugby that had for years been played in Wales and England. Still, it wasn't a far cry from "kicking a pig's bladder in skylarking fashion after Thanksgiving dinner," as Camp described early football in America.

As the *Harvard Advocate* said in 1874, the Boston Game was much better "than the somewhat sleepy game now played by our men."

In 1876, however, Princeton and the University of Pennsylvania still competed under soccer rules, while Harvard and Yale competed under the modified Boston Game. Something had to be done.

The four schools held a convention on November 26, 1876, in Springfield, Massachusetts, and formed the Intercollegiate Football Association. The Harvard boys convinced the group to adopt the

Boston Game. It was far more compelling. It simply asked the players to do more in more wide-open space.

For the next six years—while the nation was undergoing rapid change in every other walk of life, and while the best and the brightest from the top eastern schools were being drawn to the wide-open opportunity of westward expansion—this new "football" game still proved to be too slow, too stodgy for the players and the fans. Indeed, there were too few of the latter.

An analysis without a byline in the *Princetonian* in 1879 offered an opinion of the game that demanded action: "Keeping the ball and working it by passing, running and rushing is superior to the kicking game now in vogue."

In the late 19ᵗʰ century, football resembled a combination of soccer and rugby before changes to the rules helped it become the game we know today.

Keeping the ball.

Working it by passing, running, and rushing.

Superior to the kicking game now in vogue.

Not bad for 1879. Blame this mystery man in Princeton, New Jersey, for America ditching soccer.

That analysis argued that adding these upgrades would make the game more competitive for the players and a more compelling story line for an American audience gaining in literacy rates and sophistication.

The writer made this simple observation, which seemed to capture what was inherently mundane and wrong about the game at the time: "One thing is certain: as long as one side has the ball, the other cannot score, and when one team kicks the ball the other team is sure to get it."

Possession, the ability to quickly advance to the ball, hold the territory, and advance—these American concepts needed to be incorporated into the European game, the writer argued. American players and, more important, American audiences wanted it.

Fans "demanded action," wrote Parke H. Davis in *Football: The American Intercollegiate Game.* "A great clamor broke out."

So, the tinkering was over. Time for dramatic change. The year was 1880. Another convention was held. This time representatives from Columbia University joined in. New York fans were among the most clamorous for change.

First thing to go: the scrum. It suggested everything that was un-American: a mass of humanity moving in no particular direction, with no particular purpose. Instead, one team was given possession of the ball, and a line of scrimmage was created—a line on the field clearly delineating which team had the ball, and which team did not.

"A scrimmage takes place when the holder of the ball, being in the field of play, puts it down on the ground in front of him and puts it in play with his foot," said Amendment #1, adopted in 1880. Okay, so it's not exactly Jeff Saturday snapping the ball to Peyton Manning. We're not there yet.

"The man who first receives the ball from the snap-back shall be called the quarter-back," the new rule stated. So here's where Manning's prototype is born. By creating the position of "quarter-back," football's founders created a man on the field who would stand out among equals (a deliciously American concept that needs plenty of interpretation, which we will come back to in Chapter 2).

That was not enough. Another convention was held in 1882, and the participants implemented a great idea, an idea completely foreign to the football/rugby/soccer players around the world: the concept of the first down. It was like somebody flipped a light switch.

Here was the new rule they created: "If on three consecutive fairs and downs a team shall not have advanced the ball five yards or lost ten, they must give up the ball to the other side at the spot where the fourth down was made."

It was a somewhat backhanded way of saying that the team with possession must advance the ball five yards or surrender it. But, more important, it meant that if the team with the ball advanced it five yards, it kept the ball and the territory it had earned and kept going—kept possession of the football.

So, that rule also established possession—another particularly American notion. But to clearly translate the American geo-political mind-set of the time to a game on the field, there needed to be one more critical change in the game: the team possessing the ball had to be able to advance it—while holding onto the territory it had already captured. That was critical: hold and advance. Or surrender.

Ah, Manifest Destiny! Now, that's something American players and spectators could embrace. Capture territory. Hold it. Advance.

Remember, this was happening at the height of the Wild West—in all its rationalized glory. Notorious bank robber Jesse James was shot by a member of his own gang in Missouri in 1882, the same year an outlaw of another kind, John D. Rockefeller, defied his critics, his competitors, and federal regulators by organizing the first oil cartel, Standard Oil Trust. The year before, President James Garfield was shot dead. Also in 1881, in Tombstone, Arizona, city marshal Virgil Earp, his brothers Wyatt and Morgan, and Doc Holliday, opened fire in the showdown at O.K. Corral. And, in 1883, Mark Twain would publish *Life on the Mississippi*.

America needed a game that had a chance to reflect this bold, multilayered panorama of experiences.

"The Rugby code was all right for Englishmen who had been brought up upon traditions as old and as binding as the laws themselves," wrote Camp. American football, he wrote, was evolving from "the nondescript running and kicking." Camp wanted to bring scholarship and rationality to the game, make the game look more like his country.

Look at what is considered the foremost artistic depiction of Manifest Destiny, the painting *American Progress* by John Gast in 1872. In the painting, American settlers, moving westward, are stringing telegraph wire with different depictions of modern transportation. Guiding them is a white-robed angel. She is holding a schoolbook. Her name is Columbia. (Just a coincidence that it was representatives from Columbia University that joined the convention of football's founding fathers in 1880 to force the changes in the rules to create a truly American game of football.) America, bursting at the seams, needed a game that had a chance to capture this haughtiness, that movement forward at all costs. In Gast's painting, Indians and wild animals flee.

Later, it's no accident that the leaders of the Military Academy at West Point, where generation after generation of young officers would be trained to fight the country's indigenous population, would become prime movers of America's game of football, passing down army tactics from Douglas MacArthur to Red Blaik to Vince Lombardi to Bill Parcells. "This obsession with field position—with territory—is a legacy of my coaching days at West Point, where we'd get free advice from every major on campus," Parcells wrote in his autobiography in 1995. (We will come back to this in Chapter 5.)

Consider this comment from W. Cameron Forbes, the grandson of Ralph Waldo Emerson: "Football is the expression of strength of a dominant race, and to this it owes its popularity and its hopes of permanence." Forbes wrote that in 1900, just after he graduated Harvard. He later served as a governor of the Philippines in the administration of President Teddy Roosevelt, who, of course, was great purveyor of the doctrine of Manifest Destiny beyond the American continent.

So, back to the simple rule change, the creation of the first down simply mirrored the nation's quest for territory. As advancing the ball became more innovative, the first down rule would be changed from five yards to 10.

Back to Gast's painting for a moment. And Mark Twain. And the O.K. Corral. All of them—a painting, the tales of traversing the mighty Mississippi, a real event of the Wild West that took on a mythical status—helped satisfy the American appetite for stories about itself.

"America had all these fundamental myths that were important to us because we had no history, no centuries upon centuries of past history that they had in Europe," said Oregon State professor Mike Oriard, a former NFL player who has written extensively about the history of American sports. "So we had to go looking for those myths, those narratives, or create them."

With these new rules changes, with the use of territorial advancement in five- and then 10-yard increments, there would be a defined structure to the game, allowing for the formation of a narrative and the creation of another set of stories to satiate the American public. And it happened almost instantly.

It was the daily press in New York, Boston, and Philadelphia—hoping to build its readership, of course—that went looking for stories on the football field. As the game opened up, it became more of a story. The characters, with the invention of the quarterback and other distinct positions, became more defined. To be sure, early sportswriters were encouraged by their editors to glorify the game's blood and violence. It was a way to sell newspapers.

But it also served another purpose. Not everybody could go fight on the frontier or whip out a pistol in Tombstone. What was happening in the capture and surrender of territory on the football field in urban settings back east was a mythological extension of what was happening from Missouri to Arizona.

"The champions of necessary roughness" in the new American game of football, writes Oriard in *Reading Football*, "were concerned that the 'free-born American college boys' might lose their instincts of their ancestral 'fighters from way back.'"

These college football games quickly gained in popularity. By the 1890s, crowds of 10,000 and 20,000 fans were routine. And interest in the game quickly migrated west. The University of Michigan, which began football in 1878, went east as early as 1881 to play the Ivy League teams. The father of the midwestern game, Amos Alonzo Stagg, created a squad at the University of Chicago, and the *Chicago Tribune* and other midwestern newspapers responded by writing about the game in all its violent glory.

Teams from the East boarded busses and headed west to play, too. And this left fans in Philadelphia and New York, now fully engaged in the stories of their gridiron heroes, starving for updates.

So, *The Philadelphia Inquirer* came up with a pretty ingenious idea—an idea that is the forefather of the American sports bar. It's not quite 12 flat screens showing every game of the NFL's Sunday Ticket. But for 1896, it would do.

The editors of the *Inquirer* took the teletype updates of University of Pennsylvania road football games—at Columbia, Chicago, and Yale—and recreated the game on what the newspaper called a "Miniature Gridiron," a diorama displayed in a picture window in the front of the building. Hundreds of football fans would gather in front of the building, waiting for the game's drama to unfold, play by play, on a replica of the field. Think of the electric football game we played as kids growing up in the '60s and '70s, except the pieces on the field were moved by hand, one by one.

That's just how attractive the narrative of the game of football had become, nearly overnight. Interestingly, there was nothing similar to the "Miniature Gridiron" for baseball, even as that sport grew in popularity. Why? There were clearly more baseball games available to attend during the spring and summer. But a baseball game goes at a much slower pace, making updates much fewer and far between. The narrative takes place at a much slower rate. Fans would probably not stand for that.

Thus, the "Miniature Gridiron" really foreshadows why America's game of football was perfectly suited for television. The picture window in the front of the *Inquirer* was shaped like the field and the action is linear—the march to gain territory, all happening in a definable rectangular space shaped like the country itself. A newspaper picture window was the forefather of the TV set—both, in essence, a mirror of American society.

The attraction: the characters acting out a drama on the field— the narrative, the story.

On September 9, 2007, the story of whether the Jets were in any position to challenge the Patriots was told in the first possession of the game. The Jets had the ball and drove cleanly toward the 50-yard line, to the doorstep of New England territory. (As I describe this play-by-play, you hear terms like *possession* and *territory*, which we now use every day in describing a football game, and now you can understand how they originated—and how uninteresting the game must have been without them!)

With four straight successful plays, the Jets had managed a first down at their own 45-yard line. That's when Teddy Bruschi took a stand. Surgeons in Boston had used a plug to fill the hole in his heart left by the stroke—a perfect metaphor for what Bruschi does on the football field. Often the last line of defense, Bruschi fills the hole, which he was doing on this sunny afternoon in the swamp of North Jersey.

The newest element of the Jets' repertoire, running back Thomas Jones, acquired from the Chicago Bears in the off-season, carried the ball up the middle. Bruschi—the title of his autobiography is *Never Give Up*—met him brutally at the line of scrimmage for a mere one-yard gain.

Bruschi's vicious tackle put the Jets in a second and long, the first of many to come. The Jets punted. And the Patriots scored 28 of the next 35 points, winning easily 38–14.

Moss—with nine catches for 183 yards and one 51-yard touchdown bomb—announced emphatically that he was back.

Brady—missing on just six of 28 pass attempts—pronounced that this would be no ordinary season.

And the Jets gained just four yards per play—shorter than the distance of the original first down rule created in 1882. Bruschi and the Patriots defense—Belichick's brainchild—had beaten down the Jets of Mangini, Belichick's protégé.

Story lines—everywhere. Including this one: in the end, the child stuck it to the man.

During the game, Mangini noticed something that the Patriots had been doing since he was in New England. On the Patriots sideline, a member of the team's staff was using a video camera to record the Jets' defensive signals, a violation of NFL rules.

Stealing the opponents' signals is fair play—until you use video equipment. Mangini knew Belichick had done this for years. He witnessed it and benefited by it. Now, he was blowing the whistle and creating a nice little epilogue to the narrative, one that was about to last the entire season: a messy, Shakespearean epic about rivalry, secrecy, and betrayal.

Just as Walter Camp pictured it.

2

"Football is the ultimate team game."

—Dick Vermeil

"You can't have the pluribus *without the* unum.*"*

—Anonymous

How Football Explains
Daniel Boone and Davy Crockett

His name is Elisha—Elisha Nelson Manning. He is the youngest of three sons, named for his father, Elisha Archie Manning, whose own father committed suicide and whose football career was a tragedy of hope defeated by circumstances.

There was some measure of justice delivered by Archie Manning's middle child, Peyton, who combined a career of gaudy statistics and one Super Bowl title to become the undisputed king of American corporate pitchmen. But Peyton's accomplishments seemed to leave the taste of inevitability, a coronation you could admire but not enjoy.

The oldest child, Cooper—pronounced with the southern shortcut in the first syllable to come out "Cupper"—was a brilliant wide receiver in high school, but a spinal disease cut his career short. And, so, it was really up to the youngest boy, Elisha, the purest descendant of his father's dreams, and his namesake, to redeem what went horribly wrong for Archie Manning. Elisha—the name, in Hebrew, means "God is my salvation."

Like Elisha in the Bible, this Eli was misunderstood. His placid eyes were interpreted as insouciance. He did not, like his demanding older brother, publicly gesture to his teammates in disappointment or anger. Indeed, playing for the Giants of New York, he showed none of the emotional range that seems to be required from Bergen to the Bronx—none of the fire of Simms, the rage of L.T., or the outspokenness of Tiki Barber, who upon his retirement questioned Eli Manning's qualities as a field general in a way that turned occasional squawking on New York sports talk radio into a constant chorus of civic heckling and complaint. The Bible says of Elisha in 2 Kings 2:23: "and as he was going up by the way [to Bethel, a hallowed place of worship], young lads came out from the city and mocked him…"

Eli Manning had wanted this—not the mocking, of course. But he certainly wanted to be the man in New York. In the 2004 NFL Draft, Manning. his father, and his agent, Tom Condon, made it clear that he would not play for the San Diego Chargers, which owned the first pick. Under the guise that the Chargers were terminally inept, Manning Inc. lobbied to land in New York, where if Eli succeeded there could be no doubt that his father's legacy was fulfilled. So, a draft-day trade was consummated: Eli Manning to New York. The Chargers got Philip Rivers.

But the price of admission to the Big Bad Apple is always high—ask anyone from Alex Rodriguez to Stephon Marbury. And Manning—winner of just about half his regular season games and no playoff games in two years—was paying it.

"Thank god he doesn't read the newspapers or watch TV," said Archie Manning. But Archie Manning does both. And perhaps feeling a bit guilty about what he has wrought his youngest child, Archie Manning is standing in the dank bowels of Giants Stadium on the second Sunday of the 2007 NFL season, by himself, in a ballcap—this former first-round pick in the pro football draft, this man who was third in the Heisman Trophy voting, a protective father.

He is like his son, too—has a gentle heart, a forgiving nature, a face that suggests none of what you would expect from what some derisively call the First Family of Football. Nothing was handed to them. They are humble sons of the South—Elisha and his son by the same name. And, in the Bible, Elisha is described as a peaceful man, "a messenger of the kindness and love of God."

But, on this Sunday, the New York Giants, already losers of their first game of the season, would be playing the god of Green Bay, quarterback Brett Favre, and his rejuvenated Packers. No time for sacrilege here. At age 37, Favre, also a son of Mississippi, was fully in the twilight of his pro football career, looking for one more chance at a championship, now standing in the way of young Eli, 11 years younger. They did not know it yet, but what was about to take place was another truly humbling experience for Elisha and his father.

For the quarterbacks of this American game of football, this was the unavoidable journey. It's the hero's journey. He is Odysseus. Only America doesn't have Homer. It has Davy Crockett and Daniel Boone, John Wayne and Luke Skywalker.

"America does not have Greek mythology, only in school," says Professor Oriard. So, America made its own. In the march west. In making movies. On the football field. The mythology of the quarterbacks on their journey. There is nothing else like it in all of sports.

This is what attracts the American sports fan to the quarterback. It is a chance to identify with a journey well defined by our cultural experiences, our history—the quarterback driving his team down the field and through the season.

How and why the quarterback position was created and evolved helps explain how football explains America.

Let's go all the way back to 1860, the year Abraham Lincoln was elected president. At a time of unprecedented political upheaval over the issue of slavery, when civil war was on America's doorstep, a man whose name we all became familiar with as kids was more concerned with how to entertain the country. Milton Bradley invented the country's first board game. He called it The Checkered Game of Life. It would later become The Game of Life.

Bradley, a true Yankee from Maine who established his little company in Springfield, Massachusetts, called his invention "a new Social Game," according to his patent application. What was interesting was how he later characterized how the game should be played—and how he was clearly articulating the mood of the country at the time.

Those playing The Game of Life, Bradley wrote, will try "to gain on his journey that which shall make him the most prosperous and to shun that which will retard him in his progress." Not everybody was a burgeoning industrialist or inventor. Not everybody was hopping on a covered wagon to brave the elements and the American Indian in the march west. So, those who stayed behind were given a game that reflected that "journey," as Bradley explained. In other words, you can play along at home, folks. Later, in explaining The Game of Life to the American public, Bradley said, "The journey of life is governed by a combination of chance and judgment."

Chance and judgment. Judgment implies the freedom to make one. Chance implies that opportunities will be presented to you. These are singularly American concepts. (Says so, right there in the Declaration of Independence: "...certain unalienable Rights, that among these are Life, Liberty and the pursuit of Happiness." By 1860, at least somebody in the country thought it was all right to invent a game about the first item on Thomas Jefferson's wish list.)

Of course, while we don't want to be too naïve or cynical here, it's important to point out the obvious: not everybody in America had these freedoms. The Game of Life was not marketed to slave families in the south. Still, without oversimplifying matters, Bradley was just a guy trying to make a buck—by trying to capture the mood of the nation, capitalize on it, and market it.

In 1860, America's love of the idea of the frontier was in full bloom—in myth and reality. While the journey west was complex and fraught with danger, the story was repackaged into a few more easily digestible themes, the most popular being one man traversing the land, taming nature and its inhabitants along the way.

In short, the essence of the American frontier myth: the hero, using what Bradley would call "chance and judgment," was going on a westward journey, all in the pursuit of American freedom. No confluence of myth and reality was greater than Davy Crockett, the man called "King of the Wild Frontier." At age 49, Crockett's journey west ended in 1836 when he died fighting for Texas at the Battle of the Alamo. Another great frontiersman was, of course, Daniel Boone, who blazed a trail through the Cumberland Gap and escorted settlers in what later became Kentucky.

Though Boone died in 1820, 16 years before Crockett, the legends of both men were constantly being revived—and rewritten. Teddy Roosevelt founded The Boone and Crockett Club in 1887. The Sons of Daniel Boone soon sprouted an off-shoot, the Boy Scouts of America.

Of course, Milton Bradley invented his game using the same principles. And Bradley wanted those playing his game to exhibit the frontier American spirit of individualism, self-preservation, the pursuit of happiness, and freedom.

His game required strategy. He thought of it as a learning tool, and a way of projecting real-life values. Bradley, in his patent application, layered on thick the old Yankee, Puritan precepts to explain his game, which, he said, was "intended to forcibly impress upon the minds of youth the great moral principles of virtue and vice."

In Bradley's words, you can almost hear Vince Lombardi: "The virtues of playing football are many. But, in the end, football is like life. It requires perseverance, self-denial, hard work, sacrifice, dedication."

We can't draw a perfectly straight line to Lombardi yet. But the story of Bradley's invention, and his explanation of why he thought it would be successful in America, helps illustrate why soccer and rugby were reconfigured to create American football, starting in the early 1880s—and beginning with the position of quarterback.

In 1891, here is what Walter Camp, the founding father of American football, wrote about the position of quarterback, which had been invented just 11 years before: "Quarter-back has, from the very outset, been a position in which a small man can be used to great advantage." That was from Camp's *American Football*, one of the first books published on the game.

Camp's vision was for one man, relying on the game's burgeoning tactics, to prevail over the brute strength of larger men, the bulwark of the game of rugby; or the mass motion of the whole team, the essence of soccer. To fully develop into something we would recognize today, those tactics would need decades of reform and rules changes. Indeed, it's important to be historically literal here. Only the foundation had been laid for the hero's journey in the game. In the 1890s, and the two decades to follow, the quarterback position on the football field was still evolving. He was not quite yet in the category of the revived legends Daniel Boone and Davy Crockett. We are a long way from Namath, Montana, and Brady.

Walter Camp and his friends were still working out the kinks. As Camp and other reformers called for a more open game, based on the rational movement of assigned positions on the field, others clung to a game that was nothing more than a brutally violent wrestling match that often resulted in a bloody pile of humanity.

Yale head coach Walter Camp was one of the founding fathers of American football.

The Philadelphia Inquirer published one photograph that captured the public perception of American football at the time. And it was not good. Robert W. "Tiny" Maxwell, a 240-pound offensive lineman from Chicago, was playing guard for Swarthmore College in a game against the University of Pennsylvania in October 1905. At the end of the game, Maxwell—who also boxed and set the Swarthmore records for throwing the hammer and shot-put— had a busted nose. His eyes, a bloody mess, were swollen shut. And his face was cut open and smashed like a butterflied hunk of filet mignon.

———

It was so bad, the "trust buster" himself decided to get into the act.

In the fall of 1905, President Theodore Roosevelt summoned representatives of three Ivy League schools—Harvard, Princeton, and Yale—for a meeting and a warning. All across America, the howls of protest were growing—the American sport of football was backsliding into its barbaric past, a slugfest of punts and pileups that resulted in gruesome injuries. Not blown knees and twisted ankles. No, we're talking about battered faces, broken ribs, bloody skulls, and at least 18 recorded on-field fatalities.

It was a time of muckraking journalism. And magazines such as *The Nation* and *Collier's* laid bare the mayhem in a series of nasty feature articles. Editorial after editorial from Boston to Chicago urged that the game be banned. Harvard had already done so once in the mid-1880s, after tales of players just routinely and repeatedly punching one another in the face to gain advantage on the field. In 1905, Columbia banned it. The game was suspended at Northwestern and Stanford.

By 1905, at the height of the Progressive Era in American politics, Roosevelt was at the forefront of industrial and land reform. He also loved sport, especially football. "The Rough Rider," the founder of

The Boone and Crockett Club, often talked about the need for the "strenuous life." He did not want to ban football. In fact, he wanted it to survive and flourish.

"With industrialization, the closing of the frontier, and the migration to the cities," writes Oriard in *Reading Football,* "the American male was cut off from the physical demands of everyday outdoor life, through which his manhood had once been routinely confirmed. Thrust into a new world where traditional masculine traits were no longer meaningful, he found vigorous outdoor sports such as football a compensating validation of his manhood."

Recognizing football as a natural extension of the frontier mentality in America, Roosevelt wanted to reform it, but not through White House edict or congressional action. So, at a crisis point for the game in 1905, he called an informal summit (over lunch) at the White House. According to notes from the meeting, Roosevelt demanded reforms while at the "same time giving the sport, if rightly played, the prestige of his endorsement," wrote football historian Parke H. Davis at the time.

Walter Camp, representing Yale, was there. "At a meeting with the president of the United States," Camp said in a statement, "it was agreed that we consider an honorable obligation exists to carry out in the letter and in spirit the rules of the game of foot-ball, relating to roughness, holding and foul play."

This is exactly what Camp wanted. He could now engineer a game that was more rational and wide-open—a game that would eventually be focused on the quarterback. Within two months, 28 colleges sent representatives to a meeting to discuss reformation of the game. The result was a new governing organization called the National Intercollegiate Football Conference, a forerunner of the NCAA, which instituted a rules committee to save the sport of football.

Reforms came immediately. The five-yard rule for a first down was extended to 10 yards to encourage a game built on speed and athleticism, instead of merely overwhelming muscle. And, most important, the forward pass was legalized.

Camp instantly recognized what this would mean, especially to the quarterback, who now controlled the tactics on the field. The quarterback could run with the ball or he could pass it. The quarterback, he thought, would fully become the field general, and would dictate how the defense responded. And the defense would have to guess, or develop its own specified tactics based on tendencies.

"Personality will be a great feature in the new game," Camp wrote in 1910. "The boys are trained to be considered a hero."

The use of the words *personality* and *hero* suggest that it's clear the founding fathers of the game understood that for football to flourish, it was important for the game to be told just as other American myths were told, and retold, from the American West and frontier. The game, they believed, was another way to preserve— and, of course, explain—the American way of life.

And, with the creation of the forward pass, the main protagonist in the hero's journey would be the man who was part pioneer, part manager. Said historian David Wallace Adams, football was "an ideal forum for creating the new American man—half Boone, half Rockefeller."

The latter half of that equation, of course, is hardly the kind of romantic character the storytellers were looking for. The general public was not going to buy newspapers with stories about a football player who reminded them of an oil baron. Indeed, the mythology of Daniel Boone, or Davy Crockett, would do just fine. Or, as Walter Camp noted, personality would be the basis of the game from here on out—individuals accomplishing feats on the field in the face of this organized mayhem.

This idea quickly caught on. Parker Brothers of Salem, Massachusetts, a competitor of Milton Bradley's, produced one of the first board games based on football called The Foot Ball Game, which came out in 1904. The game itself contains very little strategy, just movement of the players on the field in a rather unorganized fashion.

By 1913, the next generation of football board games had the word *quarterback* in the title. Olympia Games of Chicago, Illinois, successfully marketed a game called Quarterback: A Game of Football Strategy. The board contained two spinners for two players and a gridiron for advancement based on what both sides spun. In 1925, a company called Littlefield, also in Chicago, sold a game called Quarterback: Brings Real Football into the Home.

The emergence of the quarterback position was also easily sold in the stories contained in mass-market dime-store magazines and novelettes. The cover art on magazines called *Football Action*, *All-American Football Magazine*, and *Thrilling Football*, routinely featured depictions of one man—usually the quarterback—struggling to survive or flourish on a football field overrun with would-be tacklers.

Take one cover of the magazine *Football Action*, which sold for 20¢ in 1939. There is a drawing of an anguished football player—just his face. The stories advertised: "The Swivel-Hipped Yokel," "The Triple-Threat Phoney," "Work-Horse and Glory," and "The Grandstand Hero." In many of these magazines and little books, the authors liberally use the word *hero* in their titles to describe the main protagonist on the football field: the quarterback.

And it was only a matter of time before Hollywood would get into the act. In fact, just 15 years after the game of football was in danger of being outlawed, the movie industry arrived on the scene to help permanently romanticize it. According to the American Film Institute Catalog of Motion Pictures Produced in the United States, there were 44 movies produced about football from 1921—the year the first one came out—to 1930. So, in just that first decade, Hollywood found that football was a perfect narrative for the screen.

And who better to portray that iron-jawed image of football manliness than John Wayne? Wayne's first known appearance in any movie of any kind is as a football player from Yale in *Brown of Harvard* in 1926. He does not appear in the credits. He also played a football player in two other movies, *The Drop Kick* and *Salute*. In 1929, Douglas Fairbanks Jr., perhaps the best known actor of his time, starred in football movie called simply *The Forward Pass*. Wayne was an uncredited extra in that movie, too.

But by the following year, Wayne, who played football at Southern Cal, was ready for his big role—as a romantic figure on the American frontier. It was only natural—from football player to frontiersman. In 1930, Wayne was cast as Breck Coleman in a movie called *The Big Trail*. The publicity tag line for the movie stated: "Breck Coleman leads hundreds of settlers in covered wagons from the Mississippi River to their destiny out west."

Over the following decades, Wayne would be America's leading man. First he portrayed real and fictionalized heroes of the frontier and the country's push westward. In the late 1940s and 1950s, quite naturally, he was cast in movies about World War II. Always, Wayne was the field general—directing the troops, finding a way out of trouble, prevailing against the odds. From the football field to the battlefield, Wayne symbolized the manly hero on America's journey—whoever and wherever that happened to be.

By the close of the 1950s, it was time for life to imitate art again, for the image to meet football reality—with another field general, by another guy named John, in a different medium. His name was John Unitas, or Johnny U. And the medium was television.

———

Trolling through Hollywood central casting to find somebody to play John Wayne in a movie, you would inevitably settle on Johnny Unitas. He was tall and angular. He had a squared-off jaw and a brush-cut, flattop Marine Corps look. His eyes were penetrating. He even had the same sort of lopsided gait. He rarely said much, but his stare meant business.

If he had not possessed a special gift to throw a football and play the position of quarterback, Unitas was born to lead men into battle. Or at the very least play a field general in a movie. He had what Tom Wolfe would later call "the right stuff."

But Unitas didn't have to do it in a movie. He did it on TV during what is considered the greatest football game ever played, the NFL Championship Game between the mighty New York Giants and the upstart Baltimore Colts on December 28, 1958, in the twilight of Yankee Stadium, with more than 45 million Americans watching at home on NBC.

With 1:56 remaining in the game, down 17–14, Unitas walked into the Colts huddle and delivered a line that only John Wayne could imitate: "We got 86 yards and two minutes. Let's get to work."

The story of the final two minutes of that game, and the ensuing sudden-death overtime—another completely American concept invented by then NFL commissioner Bert Bell in the dining room of his suburban Philadelphia home—have been told and retold, over and over again. And, in almost every retelling, the language is the same—it's the story of a hero's journey, against all odds, to prevail on the football field fraught with unimaginable dangers. Here's Michael MacCambridge in his authoritative *America's Game*: "The game pitting the Giants, the league's marquee franchise, against the young Colts squad led by their quietly charismatic quarterback, had taken on the aspect of grand struggle."

With the largest television audience to watch a sporting event in American history tuned in, Unitas led the Colts on not one, but two scoring drives. First he tied the game with the 86-yard drive. Then, in sudden-death overtime, Unitas drove the Colts to the one-yard line with a dazzling mix of runs and deadly accurate passes. Baltimore

Johnny Unitas was the prototype for quarterbacks in the 1950s and helped the Baltimore Colts win the greatest game ever played in 1958.

fullback Alan "the Horse" Ameche plunged into the end zone, and the Giants were vanquished in the citadel of American sports. The symbolism could not have been more perfect, or more powerful.

What Camp envisioned had reached its dénouement. Many have suggested that what Unitas and the Colts had done on national television represented a revolution in American sports. Not really. The nation had already fallen for the narrative of the game. What Unitas did was tell it with practically the whole country watching. It was great theater and great timing. The hero's journey of Walter Camp had found its greatest protagonist, a real-life John Wayne character.

And what the people watching Unitas at home saw was the same narrative portrayed in those "Miniature Gridirons" in the front of *The Philadelphia Inquirer* building. Same dimensions, same story, same audience—only bigger. As a show, the game on television was the "Miniature Gridiron," the board games, novelettes, and the early movies all wrapped up into one complete, moving, dynamic package.

After the 1958 championship game, the legend of Unitas as field general grew in stature. Reporters later found out that during the drive in overtime, Baltimore head coach Weeb Ewbank had told Unitas on the sideline to just run the football and put the Colts in position for the game-winning field goal. The domineering Ewbank did not want to risk an interception. The defiant Unitas ignored him. At the time, coaches and quarterbacks struggled to see who called the plays. Unitas saw himself as the field general. He did not like any interference with his autonomy. But, remember that Unitas was just 25 years old at the time, just three years removed from being inexplicably released by the Pittsburgh Steelers. To defy Ewbank in this grand a moment took some real chutzpah.

And, on the final play to set up Ameche's game-winning run, Unitas dropped back to pass. And his pass was perfect. He hit end Jim Mutscheller along the right sideline. Mutscheller landed out of bounds at the one-yard line.

Unitas was asked about the advisability of that pass to Mutscheller, considering that it put the Colts in unnecessary jeopardy of losing the football to the Giants at a critical juncture of the game. Reporters reminded him that the ball could have been intercepted.

Unitas replied, "When you know what you're doing, they're not intercepted." Matter-of-fact confidence delivered in a simple declarative sentence. Remind you of anybody? About 15 months later, John Wayne starred in a new movie that was a runaway hit: *The Alamo*. Wayne played Colonel Davy Crockett.

In 2003, the winner of the Johnny Unitas Golden Arm Award, given to the nation's top collegiate senior, went to Eli Manning of Ole Miss. And if that wasn't enough, when then-Giants general manager Ernie Accorsi engineered the draft-day trade that brought Manning to New York, the name Unitas was invoked over and over again. Why? Accorsi started his career as a public relations assistant with the Colts. He watched Unitas practice and play.

Once, in the late 1960s, Accorsi was watching Unitas throw the football in pain. The great quarterback had a damaged elbow. On the sideline, Accorsi was standing next to a scout named Milt Davis, a former All-Pro defensive back. Davis and Accorsi were having a conversation about the future of the team with their suddenly disabled star quarterback. "This is how you judge a quarterback," Davis told Accorsi. "Can he take the team down the field with the championship on the line and get it in the end zone?"

That quote perfectly articulates Walter Camp's vision: the narrative, the quarterback on the hero's journey, the field or the frontier to be conquered.

For Eli Manning, it also was a perfect window into the thinking of the man who drafted him with Unitas in mind. This is how Manning would be judged: as a field general in a championship game. Anything less would be failure. And, in Week 2 of year three of Eli Manning in New York, that's exactly what it was beginning to look like—a mistake. Manning, a year older than Unitas had been on that fateful day in Yankee Stadium, was struggling, again. But on this Sunday, Manning's play was standing in stark contrast to one of the game's elder statesmen, Brett Favre, who was still getting it done at the age of 37.

With the Giants Stadium crowd in stunned silence, Favre neatly spliced together scoring drives of 71 yards, 51 yards, 80 yards, 22 yards, and 53 yards. With a fastball that had a sudden, sneaky burst of speed as it reached the wide receiver, Favre completed all but nine of his astounding 38 attempts and threw three touchdown passes. Manning could only look on in awe, Accorsi in horror.

Ten weeks later, in a game several days after Thanksgiving Day, Manning performed so badly that Accorsi abandoned his second-tier Giants Stadium press box perch at halftime and went home, too embarrassed perhaps to continue watching.

On this Sunday, Accorsi stayed until the final score was posted and the fans could be heard turning grumbles into boos. Packers 35, Giants 13.

After the game, outside the Giants locker room, family members gathered in knots—children laughing, running around and crying, while wives and girlfriends waited for the Giants players to get dressed, address the shell-shocked New York press corps, and slide out of the stadium to the trash-strewn parking lot.

Archie Manning stood by himself, waiting for his son to emerge. His face was strangely placid. He's seen this movie before. He starred in it. No one was more equipped to counterbalance the narrative, to keep the story in perspective.

"We'll be all right," he said. "Eli will be just fine."

———

Interesting postscript: Remember the name Robert "Tiny" Maxwell, the Swarthmore offensive lineman who became the poster child for the modernization of American football in 1905? He had a brief playing career after Swarthmore, suiting up for the Canton Bulldogs, one of the first professional teams. But after being a last-minute fill-in as a game official, Maxwell fell in love with officiating. Ironically, the man who had been a national symbol for the brutality of football eventually led the movement for fair and honest play. Maxwell was such a fine referee, he officiated Army-Navy and Harvard-Yale games. His apartment near City Hall in Philadelphia became a mecca for game officials and

3

*"I think everybody should huddle about every 30 seconds,
kind of see how things are going. You know, 'here's our
next plan.'"*

—Steve Young, Hall of Fame quarterback

How Football Explains
Alexis de Tocqueville

The Dallas Cowboys were stuck in traffic.

Like a runaway convoy of grain trucks, the early October
wind from Lake Erie tore through suburban Buffalo, where
the streets were swallowed by long snakes of cars, minivans, pickup
trucks, RVs, and buses—all headed to Ralph Wilson Stadium, the
unlikely site of *Monday Night Football.*

Dusk was beginning to roll over the low hill country along
the lake, where gray and black clouds gathered, threatening that
a nasty downpour would hit the stadium just as the Cowboys
arrived. All of this—the rain, the traffic jam, and the mere
fact that the schedule-makers probably laughed out loud at
the thought of sending the high and mighty Cowboys to this
nearly forgotten outpost of the National Football League—was
just about all Jerry Jones could handle. Jones does not like to be
late—ever, for anything. And, in the bus, going nowhere at no
miles per hour near the godforsaken corner of Mile Strip and
Abbott Roads in Orchard Park, New York, the owner's charisma,
patience, and the creases in his well-pressed blue suit were all

getting tested. Didn't these folks up here know anything about southern hospitality?

Luckily, his quarterback, Tony Romo, seemed completely oblivious to the situation. This was Romo's way. His Cowboys ballcap was pulled way down and backward over his forehead, and his face was flush with a boyish charm. He was tossing the football around the field, testing his arm against the wind, waiting for the rest of the team to arrive, although the look on his face suggested that if they didn't, he would play the game without them. That's just the way he always is—ready for anything, anytime.

Romo had never played in Buffalo before. Didn't matter. He was already enjoying his redemption from the botched hold on a field goal in the playoffs in 2006, riding high with four straight wins to begin the 2007 season, scoring a gaudy 38 points per game, making Jones proud that the team gave him a $60 million contract, taking a chance on keeping Terrell Owens and letting Romo's mentor, Bill Parcells, ride off to Saratoga, where he could bet on the ponies, and take the lazy drive to Bristol, Connecticut, to appear occasionally on ESPN, while conspiring to find an entry point back in the league. (He took a job running the Miami Dolphins.) "Pro football," Parcells once said, "is a powerful mistress."

And Parcells loved Romo. Nothing rattled him. In another age, at another time, Romo had the personality to be a real cowboy. He likes to work, but isn't afraid to party. Other players gravitate toward him, especially when the pressure is on. Max McGee, the late, great Green Bay Packers wide receiver, who scored the first touchdown in a Super Bowl, once said, "When it's third-and-10, you can take the milk drinkers, and I'll take the whiskey drinkers—every time." Later in the season, after the Cowboys had won the NFC East, Romo would take a week off in Mexico with his girlfriend, Jessica Simpson, whose wholesome cowgirl image has been carefully crafted by Hollywood. But that little party south of the border wouldn't go over so well. On this night, Romo, however, was about to face a different kind of storm.

He seemed about as ready as any quarterback in pro football history—until the opening kickoff.

Dick Jauron, a purposeful New Englander who dresses like his wife picks out his clothes from the L.L. Bean catalog, was frankly a bit sick and tired of all the national chatter about the Cowboys. And about six minutes into the windswept game, it was clear Jauron was going to take it out on Romo. From every angle, Jauron—a crafty designer of defense—brought his pass rush after the Cowboys quarterback, relentlessly, ferociously, violently. And twice in the first half, the Bills turned interceptions into touchdowns. By the time the skies turned pitch dark and the fans from across northwestern New York had reached a full-throated frenzy, Romo had been picked five times and lost a fumble, and the Bills were cruising into the fourth quarter with an improbable 24–13 lead. In the *Monday Night Football* booth, Ron Jaworski was dumbfounded and Tony Kornheiser was stoking the impending nationally televised embarrassment about to be served to Romo, his owner, and the fun bunch from Dallas who thought this little excursion to Buffalo was going to be like a weekend trip to the Poconos. Jerry Jones, some smart aleck in the press box suggested, should've stayed stuck in traffic.

But Jones—though standing nervously in the visiting owners box—was not about to lose faith in his fun-loving, gunslinging, baby-faced quarterback. Especially not now. This is why he paid Romo all that money. This is where Jones expected Romo to earn it. And earn it, he did. Romo led the Cowboys on three scoring drives in the fourth quarter, including an 80-yarder that ended with Romo hitting Patrick Crayton with a four-yard touchdown pass with just 20 seconds left on the clock.

The Cowboys converted an onside kick, and, with two quick completions, Romo put his kicker—rookie Nick Folk—in position to strike the game-winning field goal, which he did, sending Romo whooping and hollering beyond the disbelieving fans in the end zone and into the Cowboys locker room, which sounded like somebody was having a party in Mexico.

About 20 minutes after delivering a perfectly sincere "aw-shucks-I-almost-blew-it" performance for the national press corps gathered in a small, dank room under the stadium, Romo—his face and arms bloodied and battered—stood in a corner of the locker room, swallowing a slice of pizza, watching highlights of his Houdini act on *SportsCenter*, like he was a 15-year-old hanging out in his buddy's basement after the game.

"I just told the guys in the huddle that we were going to come back and win this thing," he said.

Said tight end Jason Witten, as he got dressed to board the team bus back to the airport (this time the Cowboys would have an adequate police escort), "In the huddle, Tony was calm as could be. Nothing gets to him. He took charge in that huddle at the beginning of the fourth quarter, and that's how we came back and won."

This is what Parcells liked about Romo from the very start. Romo could command the huddle. Take charge by his mere presence. Infuse a sense of calm and energy all at once.

The huddle.

It's a sanctuary in the middle of a maelstrom. A place to take stock, make a new plan, and make a promise: to believe in that new plan and deliver it.

There's nothing else like it in all of sports. Not in hockey or basketball, or track and field or tennis. Definitely not soccer. Sure, in baseball, there is a meeting on the mound. But normally, that involves just the pitcher and the catcher. Sometimes, the infielders will join in. But most of the time, it's a stall tactic—to give the relief pitcher enough time to warm up. And it's not an encouraged or integral part of the game. No, it's a distraction, often broken up by an umpire, huffing and harrumphing as he approaches the mound.

In the American game of football the huddle is a sovereign place. It is a place where the quarterback becomes the field general, meeting with his peers, who in that moment could tell whether he had the goods to deliver them from crisis, or not.

"I think in football, because of the brutality of the sport, it lends itself to the need for a huddle, a place where you can reaffirm the notion that we are all in this together and if you listen to this next plan, we will survive," said Troy Aikman, who won three Super Bowls with the Cowboys in the 1990s. "Football is not a sport where you sit around between quarters and chew on sunflower seeds. It's intense for 60 unforgiving minutes. And the huddle helps bring us closer together. And it's up to the quarterback to convey that, but in a commanding way. You must take command."

It is establishing that understanding of leadership that determines whether a team will believe, or not—whether it will execute, or not.

"Sometimes you don't have to say a thing," said Aikman. "The other players can tell just by looking in your eyes."

It is no wonder, then, that even though the huddle was put into common practice by a very famous coach, it was created by a quarterback who happened to be deaf.

The American game of football caught on so quickly in the 1880s and 1890s that just about every college and university on the East Coast founded a team, even schools for the disabled. One of the first was Gallaudet University in Washington, D.C., which offered higher education for the deaf.

After several successful seasons, Gallaudet's fledgling football program fell on hard times until the arrival in 1892 of an innovative student named Paul D. Hubbard, who played quarterback.

When Gallaudet played nondeaf clubs or schools, Hubbard merely used hand signals—American Sign Language—to call a play at the line of scrimmage, imitating what was done in football from Harvard to Michigan. Both teams approached the line of scrimmage. The signal caller—whether it was the left halfback or quarterback—barked out the plays at the line of scrimmage. Nothing was hidden from the defense. There was no huddle.

Hand signals against nondeaf schools gave Gallaudet an advantage. But other deaf schools could read Hubbard's sign language. So, beginning in 1894, Hubbard came up with a plan. He decided to conceal the signals by gathering his offensive players in a huddle prior to the snap of the ball.

"Paul Hubbard first utilized the huddle in an attempt to conceal play calling while playing a game against another deaf team," said Ed Hottle, the head football coach at Gallaudet University. "One important thing to keep in mind is an understanding of deaf culture and deaf communication. Communication then and now is through the use of American Sign Language (ASL). It is a visual language. There is little or no privacy when communicating in public places.

"If I am signing to a player on the field during a practice, for example, all of the other players are able to know exactly what I am saying from any distance within eye shot of me and the player. If I need to speak privately to a player or coach during practice, we must either move to a secluded area or conceal our conversation by turning our backs to the team, to prevent them from seeing what we are saying. One good example: I was discussing a non-football-related issue with an assistant coach back in 2005. It turned up on a blog the next day! It didn't come from me or the assistant coach, and later we learned that someone who was sitting in the stands watching practice observed the entire conversation. The visual nature of ASL would be in my mind exactly what Hubbard was attempting to conceal from the other deaf team."

Hubbard's innovation in 1894 worked brilliantly. "From that point on, the huddle became a habit during regular season games," states a school history of the football program. In 1894, Gallaudet played two more games against schools for deaf students, the Pennsylvania and New York schools for the deaf. Gallaudet won both by a combined score of 44–6.

At that time, such prolific scoring was considered uncommon, especially at small Gallaudet. The average size of the Gallaudet line was 20 to 30 pounds lighter per man than their opponents, according to the school's history of the football program. But Hubbard's huddle innovation proved to be vital in outsmarting the opposition.

Said one coach of Hubbard at the time, "It was not generally known that Hubbard was frail in build, ill-suited for football playing. I never saw Hubbard come into contact with an opponent or dive at a fumble. He overcame his frailty with his uncanny instinct for signal calling and in handling the ball."

The Gallaudet Bison were so good they were invited to play Princeton and Yale. It was a great honor—a school for the deaf playing against Ivy League competition, at that time the best in the country. In 1895, with Hubbard at the helm, the Gallaudet team was all set to travel to Yale, which even offered a guarantee of $700 to make the trip. Legend has it that the team was willing to accept the trip under one condition—that the Gallaudet faculty purchase tombstones for the players. That's how badly they thought they were going to get beat. The team manager eventually turned down Yale's invitation, thinking the president would not approve it. The president had already turned down the trip to Princeton. But just getting invited was proof they were good.

In 1895, Gallaudet finished 5–1–2, with one tie coming at the University of Virginia, 16–16. And Hubbard's use of the huddle was getting wider exposure.

In 1896, the huddle started showing up on other college campuses, particularly the University of Georgia and the University of Chicago. At Chicago, it was Amos Alonzo Stagg, the man credited with nurturing American football into the modern age and barnstorming across the country to sell the game, who popularized the use of the huddle and made the best case for it.

Stagg was the head football coach at Chicago from 1892 to 1932. Early on, the rest of the Big Ten started to imitate Stagg's idea. And soon, to copy Stagg's success, teams all over the country began abandoning signal calling at the line of scrimmage and adopted the huddle. Remember, at the time, coaches were not permitted to send in plays from the sideline. So, while Stagg clearly understood the benefit of concealing the signals from the opposition, he was more interested in the huddle as a way of introducing far more reaching reforms to the game.

Before becoming a coach, Stagg wanted to be a minister. At Yale, he was a divinity student from 1885 to 1889. That's where he met Walter Camp, Yale's football coach. Stagg played end, making the first All-America team. After Yale, Stagg went to what was then called Williston Seminary in Easthampton, Massachusetts. While studying to become a preacher, Stagg coached the football team and fell in love with it.

When John D. Rockefeller endowed the University of Chicago with millions from his oil riches, the new president of the school hired Stagg to modernize athletics, making him one of the first paid college coaches. (He got the same salary as a professor at Chicago in 1891.)

"To me," wrote Stagg, "the coaching profession is one of the noblest and most far-reaching in building manhood. Not to drink, not to gamble, not to smoke, not to swear, to be fair-minded, to deal justly, to be honest in thinking and square in dealing, not to bear personal malice or to harbor hatred against rivals."

Thoughtful, pious, and righteous, Stagg brought innovations to football as an attempt to bring a Christian fellowship to the game. He wanted his players to play under control, to control the pace, the course, and the conduct of what had been a game of mass movement that often broke out into fisticuffs.

Stagg viewed the huddle as a vital aspect of helping to teach sportsmanship. He viewed the huddle as a kind of religious congregation on the field, a place where the players could, if you will, minister to each other, make a plan, and promise to keep faith in that plan and one another.

What is the huddle but a meeting, a place for the citizenry to gather and regroup? And what is more American than that? Our founding fathers put it right in the Bill of Rights: Congress shall make no law prohibiting "the right of the people peaceably to assemble."

The right of the people to assemble in peace really has its roots in autonomous religious congregations outside the papal authority in Europe, beginning with the changing shape of religion in Scotland. With Catholicism and the power of the pope repudiated, the Scots localized government control through something called the Kirk. "Under this concept, the only head of the church was Christ, who was not represented by a pope, but by local ministers elected by the church members themselves," writes James Webb, now a U.S. Senator from Virginia, in his landmark book *Born Fighting: How the Scots-Irish Shaped America*. "Every individual was to be held responsible for his own actions, and the church elders would be fierce in enforcing notions of 'godly discipline.'" The Scots-Irish "and other dissenting mountain communities," Webb writes, were a major factor in the creation of the First Amendment to the Constitution.

The Scots-Irish Presbyterian tradition (nearly 400,000 Scots-Irish immigrated to America from about 1750 to 1850) helped govern the American frontier. Webb writes: "...the bottoms up populism of the Kirk contrasted with the demand for strong leaders inherent in the Celtic military tradition combined to create a unique form of frontier democracy." Frontier democracy is the perfect way to describe what happens on a football field.

Webb concludes that "organized religion led by strong ministers was the backbone of the communities, for without it many would simply regress into the decadence and the spiritual emptiness of the wilderness."

Substitute *football* for *religion* and the comparison is obvious. Without Stagg, a man who was trained to be a minister, and others, the game of football might not have advanced beyond its primitive stages as quickly as it did—or, at the very least, its growth and popularity would have been stunted. Or, in the worst-case scenario suggested around 1905, the game might have been prohibited, as many college presidents were threatening to do.

By reverting to his religious roots, Stagg was attempting to modernize the game of football, using American concepts of religious discipline, democracy, and personal responsibility.

The creation of the huddle fit into this model. How? In the 19th century, Americans were using their religious and political freedom to congregate, to meet—to peaceably assemble as a way to achieve sovereignty and, of course, to prosper. It was not only Presbyterians using this model, but other religions, too. The frontier was spread out, isolated, and violent. The settlers needed community and organization to survive and flourish. ("...football, because of the brutality of the sport, it lends itself to the need for a huddle, a place where you can reaffirm the notion that we are all in this together and if you listen to this next plan we will survive," Aikman said.) The Methodists used what they called "camp meetings," holding hundreds of them annually not only on the frontier, but also in rural and farm areas. "They provided welcome opportunities for socializing and the exchange of news" and ideas, writes historian David Walker Howe in *What Hath God Wrought*.

Alexis de Tocqueville documented Americans' propensity toward association in Democracy in America.

The first man to document the extent of this widespread American phenomenon was Alexis de Tocqueville. Tocqueville, a "comparative sociologist" from France, traveled extensively throughout the United States of America in the early 19th century to try to determine how the ideas of a brand-new nation had manifested themselves into practices and institutions. And in his seminal and widely quoted book, *Democracy in America,* which was published in 1835, Tocqueville dedicates an entire chapter to how the citizens of this new country were drawn to associate, to meet, to congregate—in a way not in practice in the Old World of Europe.

The opening of Chapter 4 reads: "Better use has been made of association and this powerful instrument of action has been applied to more varied aims in America than anywhere else in the world."

Tocqueville says this propensity toward association, which is not found in his home continent, is what drives Americans in their political, economic, and religious lives, beginning at an early age, in schools, with the games children play. "Even in their games," he wrote, children "submit to rules settled by themselves…"

Tocqueville was observing, and of course at the same time celebrating, a keenly American concept: the innate right to autonomously control the course of their lives. This seems oddly commonplace, now. But you've got to remember, Tocqueville was writing this in the 1830s. He had come from Europe, where, of course, citizens were still struggling to secure the rights that Americans were now enjoying in their second generation. He wrote, "The most natural right of man, after that of acting on his own, is that of combining his efforts with those of his fellows and acting together."

Those words could easily have been uttered by Amos Alonzo Stagg, talking about the advantages of playing American football. Tocqueville recognized that from the First Amendment, Americans draw the spirit of association not yet felt in Europe, and that this helped the inhabitants of the New World in every part of their lives. "An association unites the energies of divergent minds and vigorously directs them toward a clearly indicated goal," Tocqueville wrote.

Stagg echoes these same words in his desire to modernize the American game of football. He understood that the huddle was a perfectly American—and evangelical—way of fostering teamwork in a game that had been tarnished by the arbitrary violence of mass movement of the Old World games of soccer and rugby, which had been systematically rejected in America from about 1880 on.

Go back to Tocqueville's description of association as a "powerful instrument of action." This is what Stagg recognized in the use of the huddle on the football field—a powerful instrument of action, an instrument of discipline, organization, and conduct, a chance for the team to regroup on its own after every play, reform its tactics, and proceed down the field in unison.

With coaching from the sideline still prohibited, Stagg was designing a smarter game than the one that had relied on sheer will and brute strength. He wanted the game to grow up. He needed disciplined players—players willing to be organized on the field by their peers in a tactically sophisticated way.

Stagg recognized too that the commercial appeal of the American game of football would grow with more and more scoring, and that more touchdowns could be generated by a wide-open game, a game more reliant on throwing the football, and through execution and deception. The use of the huddle allowed Stagg and his contemporaries to become more experimental and detailed in their design of passing offenses.

"Stagg brought out of the West a decidedly advanced style of play," said game founder Walter Camp. Recognizing he had something to sell, Stagg barnstormed with his University of Chicago football teams, exporting his style of play, especially to California, where college teams quickly adopted his methods and play design.

But Stagg was also the first Pete Rozelle. It was Stagg who sold the idea of the annual Thanksgiving Day game—between the University of Chicago and the University of Michigan—to Chicago newspapers as a potentially big event. He had the vision to marry football to that most American of holidays. One hundred years later, all across America, football on Thanksgiving Day—from sandlot neighborhood rough-touch games to the national TV broadcasts in Dallas and Detroit—is just as important as the turkey coming out of the oven.

No on-the-field action demonstrates America's belief in the right to free assembly better than the football huddle.

On the field, he saw to it that the game changed, too, keeping in mind that the American audience needed constant stimulation to come back for more. In 1897, Stagg introduced line shifts. A year later, he invented the lateral pass. In 1899, it was the man in motion. Five years later, he was the first to put his backfield in motion. In 1913, with these innovations making players more and more specialized, Stagg was the first coach to give his players a number on their jersey. This helped individualize the players, especially the signal caller. And Stagg pushed more and more for the use of the forward pass, thus eventually making the quarterback the most recognizable player on the field—and, thus, the most important man in the huddle.

Prior to the use of the huddle, the quarterback or another signal caller would just bark out the play as the team was reorganizing at the line of scrimmage. It was not like today's use of the no-huddle offense. Not like Peyton Manning coming to the line of scrimmage, surveying the defensive alignment, the shifting defensive players, gesturing to his line, his backs, and his wide receivers—sometimes merely for effect. No, this was done in a constant state of mass motion.

Stagg saw the limitations. With the huddle, Stagg had a way for his quarterback to control the game as "a powerful instrument of action"—just as Tocqueville recognized in the rest of American society.

And as a powerful instrument for bonding like nothing else in sports. "It's a metaphor for life," said Hall of Fame quarterback Steve Young. "There should be a family law, every family should huddle every 30 minutes."

The huddle has gone through a handful of adjustments, but it always reverts back to its original intent—even in today's game with the reliance on the no-huddle offense. The game may be more fast-paced, the defenses more apt to be confused. But most of the time—unless it is run by a master tactician like Johnny Unitas (who called his own plays) or Joe Montana (who had the instincts of a magician)—the no-huddle has the feel of an organized fire drill. And that can often interrupt the natural flow and appeal of the game. When we go to the movies, we don't want somebody constantly fast-forwarding to the "good parts." It sort of takes away from the purpose of paying to see the drama, or the narrative, unfold.

"Like mystics or ancient philosophers, we long to perceive the secret and idiosyncratic pattern within the chaos, the singular currents running through the tumultuous sea," *New Yorker* movie critic David Denby once wrote.

There was the so-called Choir Huddle, popularized by the late Kansas City Chiefs head coach Hank Stram, where the quarterback would have his back to the line of scrimmage, standing straight up, addressing the other 10 offensive players as if he were conducting a church choir. But, of course, the Choir Huddle had to be abandoned because the quarterback's lips were being read from the sideline, often telegraphing the play to the opposition.

Indeed, the "Choir Huddle" undermined the quarterback in his role as field general, generating his plan of action in secret.

In the 1970s, players started holding hands in the huddle. This was supposed to be a show of solidarity. But it appeared to be too literal—the huddle did not need to reaffirm its purpose. And besides, it did not look masculine.

"When holding hands was big, we'd get in the huddle and we tried to hold hands," said former Redskins quarterback Joe Theismann, "and some of the linemen would look at us and say, 'Don't you dare hold my hand.'"

In the end, holding hands just wasn't necessary. The huddle was best left alone to be its own interpretation of how football explains America.

"Something goes on in the huddle that's magic," said Bill Curry, the former Pro Bowl center for the Baltimore Colts. "You take a huddle on a football field and it's made up of black children and white children, and northerners and southerners, and liberals and conservatives. And not only are they forced to get along but to help each other. Here we are in the same colored helmets and the same colored jerseys and this crazy coach is screaming at us and a strange thing happens. Men become brothers."

———

Interesting postscript: Gallaudet University no longer uses the huddle on the offensive side of the ball. "Simply put we don't need it," said Coach Hottle. "We sign better than anyone in the world. We can communicate openly without too much concern about signal stealing. Installing a no-huddle offense allows us to put defenses in an uncomfortable situation. Traditionally, people huddle after most offensive plays. Utilizing the no-huddle we put them into unfamiliar territory and force them to do something they would not normally do. I have been asked many times, 'What if someone on the other team knows ASL?' I respond the same way every time: 'Good for them.' In Division III college football today, if a team can effectively steal our signs, translate them to the numbering and play calling system, translate those numbers and phrases to actual play recognition, teach that to their team in five days, have their team recognize those signs performed at very high speeds, call the appropriate defense in 25 seconds, and execute that defense, well they deserve to win! My personal feeling is that it is not possible. They would have better luck watching film. Hence we no longer huddle."

4

"When you hear my music, it's like a touchdown."

—Cordozar Calvin Broadus Jr. (a.k.a. Snoop Dogg)

How Football Explains
John Coltrane and
Jackie Robinson

Tony Dungy had wigged out and he wasn't happy about it.
You could just tell by the way he moved. Dungy, the first African American head coach to win a Super Bowl, protects his stoic public image better than DiMaggio. But on this morning he was pacing, quietly pacing like a nervous tiger, along the sideline of the RCA Dome field in downtown Indianapolis, watching his team, the current world champion Colts, try to find any kind of rhythm prior to today's game, which had been quite correctly characterized as an opportunity for redemption—not only for the team, but for the coach himself. Not that it's fair at all that Dungy would need to be redeemed from anything by anybody. But this is the week-to-week long-time-listener, first-time-caller world of the current National Football League—this is what you sign up for, expect, and must deal with.

"You can't let your emotions control what you do," Dungy said. But, oh, they do, and that's what is so attractive about the game. "Football is," former coach Marty Schottenheimer once said, "a game of the heart."

So, let us flash back to the flash point: a sloppy night at Jack Murphy Stadium in San Diego, the incandescent Peyton Manning, falling behind early 23–0 to the Chargers, brought the Colts back to the brink of pulling off a messy, rain-soaked comeback. The Colts began the game without six starters—all unavailable due to injury. Injuries claimed three more starters during the game to the point where Manning's blindside was manned at the tackle position by a guard whose name he could barely pronounce—Michael Toudouze—and who had been signed to the roster the day the team arrived in California for the game. But there was Manning, with this hodgepodge lineup, still firing, and the Colts were down by just two points in the fourth quarter with a chance to win. But—after a bad spot by the line judge and a bad call by the back judge—the Colts had to settle for a field-goal attempt, which the most reliable place-kicker in postseason history, Adam Vinatieri, missed. So, Dungy lost it—went off on the referee, Terry McAulay, on national television.

After the embarrassing walk off the field, in the locker room, Dungy did the kind of thing that has made him a unique character in the history of professional football. He apologized to his team.

"What makes him great," said center Jeff Saturday.

And now, one week later, you could just tell that Dungy was stewing. Not about the apology, but about the way he had acted and especially about the way the team lost. Before taking the field for warm-ups, he told his team something he learned from Pittsburgh Steelers head coach Chuck Noll and had repeated to his players many, many times: "Focus on the job, not the surroundings."

On this Sunday in November, the 11th week of the 2007 season, the job was simple enough: beating the Kansas City Chiefs, coached by one of Dungy's closest friends—Herm Edwards—to its current state of mediocrity. Still, Dungy paced the sideline, looking for any clue that this disparate group of athletes had found any semblance of unity, any hint of teamwork—intently studying his players, who represented the kaleidoscope of racial, ethnic, and economic backgrounds that make up pro football in America.

There was Raheem Fukwan Brock, a 275-pound defensive tackle, born in Newark, New Jersey, who went to Temple University and brought his North Philadelphia straight-up street smarts with him to the Midwest. And Rocky Michael Boiman, a thick-necked linebacker born in the Midwest, who attended St. Xavier High School in Cincinnati and went to Notre Dame. And alongside Boiman is Gary Brackett, a linebacker from Rutgers University, who brings his full-blown, full-throated East Coast attitude to every game. And there is quarterback Peyton Williams Manning of New Orleans, first son of the first family of football, throwing darts to his trusted battery-mate, wide receiver Reggie Wayne, also of New Orleans, who went on to the University of Miami. Manning is from the University of Tennessee, but his unabashed competitiveness often overpowers the genteel charm taught by his father and mother, true children of the South. Wayne, soft-spoken in public, was schooled in that ferocious South Florida hothouse of football that has its own brand—The U. More than 75 percent of the NFL's players are African American. But those from the University of Miami—Ray Lewis, Ed Reed, Reggie Wayne, Kellen Winslow, Vince Wilfork, Santana Moss, his brother Sinorice, Clinton Portis, Warren Sapp, and on and on—stake claim to the top rung. Being from The U is a kind of hip-hop shorthand, binding a brotherhood that inhabits the highest echelon of an unofficial ruling class of African American players that dominates pro football. It is built on speed and physical power, mental toughness, and an impenetrable single-minded fraternity of protection. Not quite a street gang, of course. But a gang nonetheless—one that often trades in the same

"Straight, No Chaser" is a Thelonious Monk composition. Monk lived on the edge of life, wrote his music around the edges of jazz. He always found the cracks in the diatonic scale. In other words, Monk mastered the fundamentals, but then he found those shades of chromatic deviation. A perfect football metaphor.

"I have been sitting on the sideline listening to that Miles Davis cut while [watching] the 49ers with Joe Montana and Roger Craig and Jerry Rice and John Taylor and Tom Rathman and you hear that piece, that 'Straight, No Chaser,'" Edwards said. "Then, all of sudden Cannonball kicks in and you hear Montana: 'Hut, hut, hut.' Then everything starts to move, and you see that rhythm. It's like Coltrane coming in and picking up pieces after Cannonball leaves off. And you hear that bass in the background. You hear Garland carrying the whole thing on piano and you see Joe handing the ball to Roger or Tom. It's all of one cloth. That's why some of the greatest American musicians are some of the greatest sports fans. They understood the game. They understood the risk. They understood the practice. You're not just getting ready to run a play during a game, you're downloading the rhythm of the play, the timing of the play, the purpose of the play, the spirit of the play into your automatic response system. So, when that play is called, you go up. You're not thinking now, you're just running the play."

Coltrane's groundbreaking solo with the Miles Davis sextet on "Straight, No Chaser" was recorded in 1958.

"Coltrane would go into his flat and practice for like 72 hours straight," said Edwards, "and it's the same way with plays. I watched the 49ers run play after play after play. It wasn't practice for practice's sake. It wasn't practice to get the play down. It was practice to make the play automatic. And it's the same way with music. That is shared. The risk, playing without a net, getting out there, trying to make it happen against competition. Competition in music being the piece itself. Asking yourself, 'Can I get this done?'"

John Coltrane's improvisational style and meticulous preparation changed the world of jazz in the 1950s and 1960s.

On this Sunday, this is what Tony Dungy—the unquestioned leader of the dominant African American culture in pro football—was looking for: whether his players were finding any kind of personal rhythm to get the Colts back on track, whether they were finding a way to connect to their automatic response systems—whether the Colts could regain the respect they thought was due, whether they could get this done.

With Snoop Dogg's "What's My Name?" playing in their headphones.

———

Of course, it was not always like this. American football—with Walter Camp out of Yale, and his protégé Amos Alonzo Stagg putting down roots in Chicago—was dominated by the upper echelons of American society in its first generation of existence. Read: white college students.

And as the game grew more complicated, the view among those who controlled football was that black players just were not smart enough to understand it. In his autobiography in *Collier's* in 1930, Notre Dame coach Knute Rockne told the story of two black teams deciding that since play calling might prove too complicated for their players, they came up with plays named after favorite dishes: "Pork chops mean a smash through right tackle. Pigs' feet a run around right end."

Even while big-time college football contained several dozen black players by the mid-1930s, these stereotypes died hard. Football magazines and novelettes at the time never used black faces on the cover or black football players as the main protagonists. The official 15¢ program from a 1935 game between San Jose State and the College of the Pacific illustrates the stereotypes that persisted even while black players were fairly commonplace on college football teams: a large, happy-faced white football player eating hot dogs that he just purchased from a Sambo-faced black vendor, who is mouthing the words, "third down and four to go." The "four" refers to the hot dogs, not yards. The upshot is clear: the blacks clearly belonged in the role of service to the game, not as participants.

Of course, a black halfback by the name of Frederick "Fritz" Pollard had already led Brown University to a Rose Bowl berth in 1915. Fritz Pollard did not have to wait for a Branch Rickey to force the integration of professional football. In 1921, Pollard led the Akron Pros—in the fledgling professional football league that had sprouted out of the factory cities and towns of the Midwest—to a championship in 1921, the second year of the league's existence.

Pollard played the position of left half back. The quarterback would bark the signals and call the plays, but the left halfback usually received the direct snap of the football and then dished it like a point guard. So, Pollard's importance to the team was critical. And he proved to be a far superior athlete, playing both ways for the Pros, handling all the kicking duties as well. He did everything—although he was not allowed to dress for the game in the locker room with the rest of the team, which was white. He dressed in a nearby boarding house. But he was so good, Pollard was named the head coach of the Akron Pros—then he was allowed to dress with the rest of the team. (Today, the organization that represents black coaches in the NFL is called The Fritz Pollard Association.)

The Pollard story illustrates that football—more than baseball at the time—explains what was happening in America. Just like the nation and its people, the game was growing so quickly, and all those messy growing pains were right out in the open: with maddeningly persistent prejudices alongside singular stories of struggle and triumph. Pollard never graduated from Brown. Couldn't cut it. But he was a trailblazer in the game of football—not only for African

Americans, but for anybody else who came from nowhere and wanted a chance to play, and perhaps make a living. He introduced an element of speed and daring—just like Jim Thorpe did for the Carlisle Indians, who beat the Cadets of West Point in 1912. The Indians did it by throwing the football—doing to the Army team what Stagg envisioned from the beginning.

As he barnstormed the country with this new game, Stagg recognized, too, that football was not going to last as a bastion of colleges and universities. He detested this new professional league developing right under his nose, but he knew that the game would have to reflect what America looked like. And what America looked like around 1920 was a country teeming with immigrants in cities like New York, Chicago, Cleveland, and Pittsburgh. So, he recruited heavily in urban and industrial areas.

"Boys from the city were more aware of their surroundings, more observant," Stagg said. "They're more alert."

And the children of immigrants gravitated toward football for a particular reason, writes professor Michael Oriard: "Whereas early immigrant groups such as the German and Irish brought their own sporting traditions to the New World, the newcomers typically did not. First-generation new immigrants were generally antagonistic to sport, viewing it as a waste of time, but their offspring embraced athletics as a key part of their new American culture and identity." For the immigrant children, being involved in sports "fostered assimilation into mainstream American culture, and the school and professional sports meant distinctly American success and more thorough absorption into the mainstream."

The story of westward expansion, although still embraced in Hollywood, was no longer the dominant narrative. And so why wouldn't the American game of football represent, and embrace, this new plotline? You see stories in the popular football press about "the Dazzling Duce from Little Italy," and "the Big Stiletto," and "Papa Morelli's Boy."

To play football, whether in high school or on a college or professional team, was to be thoroughly American. Polish and Italian youths "were simply drawn to football in high school as a vehicle for achieving status," writes Oriard. "College coaches grabbed them not as aliens to be Americanized but as rugged and hungry football players."

Of course, this was the early 1900s. Only a handful of immigrant boys had access to college. So, finding places to play football beyond high school, where the game was also just being embraced on a widespread basis, was difficult. Small amateur football clubs, dating back to the 1890s, were confined to the state of Pennsylvania. The earliest may have been the YMCA squad from Latrobe, near Pittsburgh, in 1895, which would often pay a nominal stipend to players who participated in exhibition football contests for crowds that could not afford to go to a college game.

"The fans at these early contests approached hysteria, either paying at the gate or throwing some change into a hat passed at halftime," according to one entry in an early football encyclopedia. "And the football fanatics in the stands charged games with life-or-death significance. The supporters of the victorious squad often piled out of the park and into the center of town in a boisterous and electric mob." Once, the courthouse steeple in Latrobe (home of Rolling Rock beer) had to be repaired because a crazed group of football fans tried to destroy it.

But passing the hat was no way to finance a football league. The Philadelphia Athletics and Philadelphia Phillies baseball teams started clubs in 1902, joining a team from Pittsburgh in a three-team professional league called the National Football League. Players from the two Philadelphia clubs combined to field a football team that traveled to Madison Square Garden in New York City to play a team from Syracuse in an indoor tournament in December. By 1903, however, the fledgling professional teams in Pennsylvania struggled to make ends meet and folded.

Ohio was next. Small professional teams were started in Canton, Columbus, Massillon, Dayton, and, of course, Akron. In 1915, Canton signed Jim Thorpe (just three years removed from his Olympic feats and his star turn with the Carlisle Indian School), for the unheard-of sum of $250 a game. The average attendance at Bulldogs games went from about 1,000 spectators to 8,000—still nothing like the crowds at football games at Michigan or the University of Chicago.

However, the folks who ruled college football knew what was happening. And they didn't like it. They saw that their game—which meant big money from big crowds—was threatened.

The American Football Coaches Association met and voted to unanimously endorse the following resolution: that professional football was "detrimental to the best interests of American football and American youth." Many conferences prohibited their football players from suiting up for a professional team. Same went for game officials.

But, to some who wanted to see the game grow, this all smacked of elitism and collusion. And there was no denying that playing football, or watching it, was a way for the children of immigrants to find an entry point into American culture, especially for those who had no access to college. So, there was a growing appetite for football beyond the college game. And it had to be satisfied. It's the American way.

World War I obviously interrupted participation in most of these small pro teams. But after the war, they quickly resurfaced and started to flourish. In 1920, with George Halas at the helm as the coach of the Decatur Staleys, the representatives from 11 football clubs met in an automobile showroom to form the American Professional Football Association in the wheelhouse of the industrial Midwest: members included the Canton Bulldogs, Massillon Tigers, Akron Pros, Dayton Triangles, Cleveland Indians, Rochester Jeffersons, Rock Island Independents, Muncie Tigers, Hammond Pros, Chicago Cardinals, and the Decatur Staleys of Halas.

The following year, Halas renamed his team the Bears, and he moved them to Chicago, proving Amos Alonzo Stagg right. Football was, indeed, a city game.

———

"When I was 10 years old I paid 10 cents to see Red Grange run with a football," wrote the late W.C. Heinz, considered one of the greatest sportswriters of his generation. "That was the year when, one afternoon a week, after school was out for the day, they used to show us movies in the auditorium, and we would all troop up there clutching our dimes, nickels or pennies in our fists.

"The movies were, I suppose, carefully selected for their educational value. They must have shown us, as the weeks went by, films of the Everglades, of Yosemite, of the Gettysburg battlefield, of Washington, D.C., but I remember only the one about Grange.

"I remember, in fact, only one shot," Heinz wrote. "Grange, the football cradled in one arm, started down the field toward us. As we sat there in the dim, flickering light of the movie projector, he grew larger and larger. I can still see the rows and rows of us, with our thin little necks and bony heads, all looking up at the screen and Grange, enormous now, rushing right at us, and I shall never forget it."

While Hollywood made football players into these characters of melodrama or comedy, there was now no getting around this fact: in the age of Babe Ruth and Jack Dempsey, there was no substitute for the real thing. In American cities busting at the seams with every possible variety of real life and real hardship, there was no substitute for the real struggle in sports. And nowhere was that struggle played out more intensely than on the football field.

But to sell it, to get kids to plunk down their dimes, nickels, and pennies like W.C. Heinz, you needed star attractions.

And the newly formed football club in the world capital of New York did not have one. The New York Giants were going out of business. Until Red Grange saved them.

The year was 1925. And Harold Edward Grange, a running back from the University of Illinois, the son of a lumber foreman from Forksville, Pennsylvania, was the biggest thing in football. Not literally. He was only 170 pounds. But he was quick and light on his feet, changing direction like a prairie wind, alluding tacklers who dove in frustration for the empty space that Grange had once occupied. It was like he had never been there, just a figment of the linebacker's imagination. Thus, his nickname: "The Galloping Ghost."

Only, to boys in cities across America, Grange was all too real—a real-life football hero whose story was told every week in movie houses in Boston, Cleveland, Chicago, and New York. The packed auditoriums were nothing compared to the stranding-room-only crowds of wild football fans that Grange attracted to college campuses: 67,000 to watch him score five touchdowns to beat Michigan; 60,000 in Nebraska; and 85,500 in Columbus to watch him play Ohio State. Remember, this was long before TVs were common in every home.

Grange was college football's big ticket. The big question in 1925, Grange's senior season, was whether the football fathers who ran the college game had convinced him to reject pro football. They wanted him to go straight to Hollywood, where his myth could be retold on the big screen in perpetuity, or to Wall Street, where the go-go '20s was sure to provide him with all the wealth he needed—anything but help build the fan base in the pros.

But George Halas had other ideas—Grange should stay in Illinois, move to the big city, play for the Bears, and help the nation's struggling new professional football league take the next step. And that's exactly what Grange did. He wanted to play football. So, he took the money.

After his last game for the Illini, Grange signed with the Bears and agreed to barnstorm—Papa Bear Halas was stealing Coach Stagg's ideas right in his own backyard—across the new league in the final weeks of the 1925 season.

On Thanksgiving Day in 1925—hey, why not totally pilfer Stagg's inventions?—Halas unveiled pro football's newest attraction. More than 36,000 paying customers showed up at Wrigley Field. What a coup—a big crowd not to watch baseball, but this struggling game of professional football.

But Grange's debut was a bit of a disappointment. The Bears and Chicago Cardinals played to a scoreless tie. Still, because of Grange, the *Chicago Tribune*, which had rarely dedicated a single column inch to pro football, covered his first game like it was a heavyweight title bout. Halas was making headlines for a league that had been considered a pariah.

Three days later, despite a snowstorm in Chicago, the crowd was just as big at Wrigley Field. This time, Grange gained a total of 140 yards rushing and receiving. The Bears beat Columbus 14–13 and the local newspapers caught what was called "Ghost Fever."

Time to take the show on the road. Big crowds followed. St. Louis was first. Then Philadelphia, where a team named the Frankford Yellowjackets struggled to attract a smattering of fan interest. At Shibe Park in North Philadelphia, 36,000 star-gazing football fans braved the heavy rains, which negated any possibility that the ghost would be galloping that day. But the crowd stayed to the end, and Grange scored twice as the Bears won 14–7.

All of that was nothing but a nice warm-up act for the big show in the big-city lights of Broadway.

For this new league to make it, for this new city game to have any chance of being viable, it needed the biggest city of them all. The Giants were founded in 1925 by a bookmaker who made his money playing the horses in Saratoga, New York—a playground for Manhattan's titans of business and industry. New York's entry into this new pro football league played its first season at the Polo Grounds, home of the immensely popular New York baseball Giants. The custodial crew at the baseball game would have outnumbered most of the football fans that showed up to watch young Tim Mara's team.

Until Sunday, December 6—that's when Papa Bear Halas brought Red Grange to the Great White Way. A record-setting crowd of 73,000 jammed into every corner of the Polo Grounds for a glimpse of the Ghost.

Grange only scored once, but it was enough to satiate the crowd and carry the Bears to a 19–7 victory. Ironically, on the same Sunday afternoon, the actual championship of Halas's league—the American Professional Football Association—was being played in Chicago. The Pottsville Maroons beat the Chicago Cardinals 21–7 in a game that was later disallowed after a protest was filed with league commissioner Joe Carr. It didn't matter. Nobody cared about the Maroons or the league title.

Just Red Grange. Indeed, after the season was ended, Carr reminded each club of one of the league's original rules: no college player could be signed before his class had graduated. Carr was just patronizing the college presidents. After all, the grand prize of the college gridiron, Red Grange, was already wearing Papa Bear Blue.

Halas had taught his new league a valuable lesson: to make it in America's new burgeoning urban empires, you needed big stars. Just like in the movies and on Broadway. The young, vibrant sons of immigrants would embrace the American game of professional football—if you gave them a hero to watch, a story to follow.

The important epilogue to this story took place 15 years later. At the University of Chicago, Stagg had retired as head coach in 1932, and for the next eight years, the football program slowly deteriorated. In 1940, with the nation on the doorstep of another world war, the football team founded by the man most responsible for creating the modern age of the game finally closed its doors. The University of Chicago stopped playing football.

———

Other doors were closed, too. The door that had allowed Fritz Pollard to enter the early pro game had been slammed shut. To this day, it's not clear why or on what exact day it occurred. But, in 1933, the National Football League banned black players. There is no meeting that anyone can point to, no documentation of how it all happened. It's a well-guarded secret to this day. In the 1920s, blacks played professional football in America. The year after Franklin D. Roosevelt was elected to his first term as president, pro football established a racial barrier. Only whites allowed.

William C. Rhoden, an author and trailblazing journalist for *The New York Times* who has studied and written about this subject for more than 20 years, believes it was simply a matter of "racial economics."

In 1926, the year after Grange's debut, Halas's league reached its pinnacle. There were 22 pro teams in 1926—from the New York Giants to the Duluth Eskimos, who featured Ernie Nevers, an All-American fullback who was coached by Pop Warner at Stanford. With Nevers and Grange now barnstorming, the league flourished. But that success was fleeting. Only 12 teams survived into 1927. When the Depression hit, pro football barely sustained itself, dropping to only eight teams in 1932, which is also the year George Preston Marshall came into the league with his Boston Braves. Marshall, who would later move the Braves to Washington and call his team the Redskins, was the last man to reintegrate his team—in 1962. The Kennedy administration forced him to do it. So, in 1932, Marshall was among the most vocal owners to bar black players. But there are no records of exactly how or when the actual act of banishment took place, according to Rhoden and others.

"The bottom line may have been that blacks were just taking jobs away from white guys," Rhoden said. "It's the same thing that happened in baseball in 1875. Jobs were at a premium. They didn't want black guys taking their jobs."

In 1939, UCLA went undefeated, carried by the singularly spectacular exploits of Kenny Washington at left halfback. Washington was considered the best college football player in the country. He was black. No professional football team signed him to a contract. Ironically, one of his backfield mates on that team was Jackie Robinson. He was never invited to play pro football. "It wasn't like baseball, where owners could argue—however disingenuously—that they had no way to know if black players could play at the major league level," said Charles Ross, an associate professor of history at the University of Mississippi. "Pro football owners watched black players like Jackie Robinson compete against their league champions in all-star games every year. They obviously preferred not to see."

The ban against black players lasted until 1946, the year before Robinson broke the color barrier in baseball. But the circumstances were quite different in football. There was no Branch Rickey like where would be in Brooklyn. Instead, when the Cleveland Rams re-located to Los Angeles in 1946, several black journalists, including Brad Pye Jr., the longtime sports editor of *The Los Angeles Sentinel,* called on the Los Angeles County relocation commission to prohibit the Rams from playing in a publicly funded facility unless they integrated. So, Washington—now seven years removed from his prime at UCLA—was given a tryout with the new Los Angeles Rams. He made the team. And in his second year in the pros—now eight years removed from his last real competition at UCLA—Washington led the Rams with 60 rushes, gaining a team-high 7.4 yards per carry.

Back in Cleveland, the Rams were replaced by a new team in a new league. Paul Brown started the new Cleveland Browns of the

Cleveland Browns running back Marion Motley helped break professional football's color barrier in 1946.

All-America Football Conference, and he wasted no time bringing in two black players in 1946. Brown was a former head coach at Ohio State and had coached a professional squad that played at the Great Lakes Naval Station north of Chicago. He knew from his experiences in college and the armed forces that integration could help him win. In August 1946, he invited Bill Willis, a black lineman who played for him in Columbus, to the Browns' first camp. Willis needed someone to room with him. That's how fullback Marion Motley got to join the team.

In 1946, while the new commissioner of the NFL, Bert Bell, was forced to deal with a gambling scandal that implicated two New York Giants in the league championship game, Brown was revolutionizing the game with speed and power, with Motley as the focal point. The Browns won the first AAFC championship that year. Brown's team thoroughly dominated the AAFC, going 47–4–3 and winning four straight titles from 1946 to 1949, when the struggling league folded.

They went 14–0 in 1948. That undefeated season was never recognized, because it happened in a defunct league. But the NFL recognized the Browns, letting them join the big boys. And they recognized the way Brown's team had changed the face of professional football. Motley, who led the AAFC in rushing, led the NFL in rushing in 1950, his first season in the league. In 1968, Motley was inducted into the Pro Football Hall of Fame.

The story of Tony Dungy's NFL career contains no less romance. There is no straight line from his promising career as a college quarterback at the University of Minnesota to that night in Miami when he held the Vince Lombardi aloft in the rain. No, his journey is like a Coltrane melody that requires every ounce of imaginative improvisation, every nuance of syncopation—and lots of humility and practice—to be complete.

Dungy grew up in Jackson, Michigan, in the late 1950s, and he played quarterback at the University of Minnesota from 1973 to 1976, finishing as the school's career leader in pass attempts, completions, yards, and touchdown passes. But he did not get drafted. And when the Pittsburgh Steelers signed him as a free agent after his senior season, head coach Chuck Noll—always blunt, but always with a plan—told Dungy he would be playing defense, not quarterback.

Noll had already taken a chance on another black quarterback, Joe Gilliam, which didn't quite work out. And with Terry Bradshaw already on the roster as the starter, Noll did not see a spot for Dungy. Nevertheless, Dungy always wondered what might have been, what should have been.

"Some people had suggested to me that I wasn't drafted as a quarterback because of my race," Dungy says. "At first, I didn't agree. I just figured that playing quarterback in the NFL was completely different from playing in college. But after talking with coaches and scouts that first year, I grew less certain. A number of them said they had passed on me in the draft because of my height and arm strength. Later in the season, however, when we played guys like Bob Griese, Joe Ferguson, and Fran Tarkenton, I would deliberately walk by, look them in the eye, and measure my height against theirs. I was as tall as each one of them. I began to wonder if race had indeed played a role. To make matters worse, when I saw the backup QBs, now that was really frustrating. A lot of them just weren't very good. I continued to wonder."

Despite those silent resentments, Dungy flourished in the NFL by learning from Noll the importance of practice and preparation—by "doing the ordinary things in an extraordinary way," as Noll would hammer home. Like Coltrane, Dungy became a meticulous practice guy and he instilled that notion in his players when he became a head coach—first in Tampa, then Indianapolis, where in 2006 he became the first African American head coach to win the Super Bowl.

I remember interviewing him on the podium in the rain in Miami after former Dolphins head coach Don Shula had handed Dungy the Lombardi Trophy. I asked him about what it meant to be the first, and he stood there for just a second as it finally sank in. "It means a lot. Right now, I have a hard time putting it into total perspective. But I know what it took to get this point—for me and all those who came before me," he said.

In that Super Bowl win, Dungy beat a protégé named Lovie Smith, the African American head coach of the Chicago Bears. A season later, on the field at the RCA Dome, Dungy was facing the Kansas City Chiefs, coached by another protégé from the ranks of minority coaches, Herm Edwards.

The Colts had no business losing to the Chiefs. But they started out slowly—it was clear that there was nothing in their "automatic response systems." Dungy's team looked listless. But the Chiefs were inept, playing a second-year quarterback, Brodie Croyle, who was overmatched. But Peyton Manning seemed to be lost, too. A 10–10 tie was broken by Adam Viniatieri's 42-yard field goal with three seconds left.

At midfield after the game, Dungy and Edwards embraced.

"I love you," said Edwards

"Love you, too," Dungy said.

5

"Americans love a winner and will not tolerate a loser.
Americans play to win—all the time."

—George S. Patton

How Football Explains
West Point

Woody Johnson is jealous.

Johnson is the owner of the New York Jets—the Big Apple's second sister of a football team. And there wasn't a day in 2007 that he came to his office at Weeb Ewbank Hall (named for the only head coach to bring the Jets a Super Bowl trophy) without being reminded with a thwack across the chops that his division rivals to the north, the New England Patriots, were orbiting in the historical mesosphere of an undefeated season, and across the Hudson River, the crosstown New York Giants were shaking off a nasty case of early-season doldrums and heading for a showdown with Tom Brady & Co. in a game that no one suspected could be a rehearsal for Super Bowl XLII. Not even Woody Johnson.

But, in Woody's world, it seemed inevitable. There was no escape. He had to ignore the newspapers. The back page of the *New York Post*: "Patriots Drop 52 On The Skins." The *Daily News*: "Big Blue Wrecking Crew." The *Star-Ledger* of Newark, New Jersey: "Gang Green Chokes On Sixth Straight Loss."

73

He had to turn off the radio. Joe Benigno, the insufferable Jets fan who became a host on New York's nonstop scream-and-shout sportsfest of a radio station—The FAN, WFAN-New York—was ranting and raving every day about Chad Pennington's arm strength, about whether Kellen Clemens was ready, about Thomas Jones's heart, and finally, but most important, asking the question everybody thought was answered in 2006: is head coach Eric Mangini in way over his head?

It is late November 2007. The Jets, after shocking the Pittsburgh Steelers at Giants Stadium the previous Sunday, have a date with the Cowboys in Dallas on Thanksgiving Day. A little holiday trip to Big D. And nobody is wondering if the Jets can make the playoffs, only whether it is possible to win two in a row—just give the fan base a little streak that also might (emphasis on *might*) resuscitate belief in the coach.

Mangini—there was never supposed to be any question about him. Here's the DNA: Parcells-Belichick-Mangini. Hard core football guy came out of the Cleveland Browns organization with Bill Belichick, who was tutored by Bill Parcells with the Giants, the Patriots, and the Jets. By age 34, Mangini had won three Super Bowls with Belichick in New England. He was supposed to be the natural heir. Learned it all from Belichick: the situational, week-to-week defensive game-planning; a ruthless all-business approach to the roster; the demands for intense physical training, precise practices, maniacal focus, and dedication to the cause—the principles of any good military organization.

That's why Woody Johnson recruited Mangini. Belichick objected. It was the wrong move, the wrong team, he told his protégé. And, besides, coaching in the same division against his old team and boss was an act of disloyalty.

But Mangini thought he was ready. Besides, they don't give these jobs out at the grocery store. There are only 32 NFL teams. Stupid to turn down the opportunity—not to mention the money. And Mangini believed it, too, that he was indeed the heir apparent to the Parcells-Belichick legacy, ready to wear the coat of arms.

And the first year at the Jets' helm seemed to confirm that. Year one, 2006. Mangini demanded loyalty and secrecy. He used all the buzz words he learned from the masters, talking about the mystic dimension of service and the sanctity of oath. Work hard, play harder, trust your coaches, and reveal nothing to the outside world, especially reporters. "You know what you guys are?" Parcells once said to a gathering of writers covering the Giants. "Communists. Subversives from within."

Parcells treated reporters with grinning ridicule. Belichick with cold silence. Mangini tried to imitate a little of both. Could not yet pull it off. Didn't have the chops or the credibility.

But in 2006, the Jets rewarded their first-year head coach with a nice little honeymoon with the press and the fans: a berth in the AFC playoffs—coin of the realm for a freshman coach. So what if Mangini had been bounced out in the first round by his old boss? He had a new nickname. The coach the players called "the Penguin," because he waddled around the practice field looking dumpy in his sweats, was now being referred to as "Mangenius." And Woody Johnson was happy. Parcells had won two Super Bowls. Belichick had three. The arc of revival had begun. By all appearances in that first season, Mangini looked like the young lieutenant with all the right gridiron genetics.

For a full understanding of that football legacy, you have to go back before Mangini's educational days in New England, before Belichick's tutelage, before Parcells landed with the Giants in the 1980s.

You have to go back to Vince Lombardi, and to the man who taught him at West Point, Earl "Red" Blaik, the coach of the last great Army football teams of the 1940s. And to understand Lombardi and Blaik, you have to start with the man who laid the foundation for it all, the flamboyant commandant at the United States Military Academy who would become known as the American Caesar.

That's right, to get to Mangini, you have to start with MacArthur—General Douglas MacArthur.

Douglas MacArthur

Other than George S. Patton, there is no figure in American military history that comes with more pomp and imagery than Douglas MacArthur. And none accomplished more. MacArthur served in three wars—World War I, World War II, and the Korean War. He accepted the Japanese surrender in 1945. He was one of only five men in history to rise to the rank of General of the Army.

And he loved sports. So, after serving with the highest distinction in France during World War I (he was the most decorated American officer in the war), MacArthur was given the assignment by President Woodrow Wilson to clean up and reform the U.S. Military Academy at West Point. Naturally, MacArthur started with the athletic department.

Upon the fields of friendly strife
Are sown the seeds
That, upon other fields, on other days
Will bear the fruits of victory.

He wrote that quatrain and ordered it carved on the stone passageway leading to the West Point gym. MacArthur liked to repeat this quote from John Dewey, considered America's first great educational reformer. "There is an impossibility of insuring general intelligence through a system which does not use the body to teach the mind and the mind to teach the body."

At West Point, MacArthur ordered the student body to participate in intramural athletics. But he went much further than that. He made trips to Washington and wrote letters to members of Congress urging them to look for gifted young athletes to appoint to the Military Academy. He lobbied for a new stadium to be built on the Hudson River where the Army's football team could play this new American sport played at Harvard, Yale, Columbia, Michigan, and the University of Chicago. MacArthur was the first to reward his football stars with special privileges. They were given elite status on campus. And there was not to be a hint of resentment. This was MacArthur, after all, and nobody was about to roll eyes at anything he did.

General Douglas MacArthur was a distinguished leader in the U.S. Army and later at the U.S. Military Academy at West Point.

And why would there be any dissent? MacArthur earned a reputation during World War I for being courageous in the line of fire. He was a soldier's soldier. MacArthur's policy during the war: "Lead men from the front." (Ever see those slow-motion NFL Films shots of Bill Parcells at the end of the Giants Stadium tunnel, ready to lead his team onto the field? He's in front. He holds his arm out, preventing anyone from breaking ranks. When and only when Parcells gives the signal do the players charge on the field behind him. That's not by accident. Lead from the front. But we'll get to Parcells.)

MacArthur himself wasn't much of an athlete. He played baseball at West Point from 1899 to 1901. Played right field, but had a weak bat. In his senior year, he joined the football team— as the manager. But when he returned to West Point after World War I, it was football that he regarded as the sport that could fulfill that quatrain he composed and desperately tried to instill into his cadets.

Remember, it was MacArthur who uttered that singularly American combat motto when he was on the front lines in France: "In war, there is no substitute for victory." (Years later, Vince Lombardi would say, "Winning isn't everything. It's the only thing." But, again, we're getting ahead of ourselves.)

Ironically, during his three years at West Point, Army lost three straight to Navy. Of course, that frustrated MacArthur to no end. Still, he had succeeded in something much larger: changing the culture at Army, instilling a dedication to the serious pursuit of athletics as a way of molding men for battle, and, most important, creating an expectation of success.

In the cool spring and fall afternoons of upstate New York, once classes let out, MacArthur liked to wander around his newly developed athletic fields to watch practice. Wearing a coat below the knee, his arms crossed behind him, he cut the figure that only he could claim, that of a general inspecting the readiness of his troops.

One of his prized cadets remembered a particular incident: "I was having trouble hitting curveballs. As usual, MacArthur had stopped by to watch the team practicing. I knew that he had been a pretty fair ballplayer in his time, so I decided to ask him for a little expert advice on batting. I wasn't too surprised, either, when the general loosened his stiff collar, took off his Sam Browne belt, and stepped into the batter's box. It must have been the only time that I ever saw him fail to accomplish something he set out to do. When it was my turn at bat again, I not only couldn't hit a curve, I couldn't even hit a straight ball."

The young baseball player taking batting tips from MacArthur was Earl "Red" Blaik.

Red Blaik

During MacArthur's tenure as superintendent at West Point, Blaik was the star athlete.

In 1921, Blaik led the baseball team to victory over Navy. To celebrate the win, he led the corps in a nighttime parade around the academy grounds, including right in front of MacArthur's residence. The whole rowdy procession was in violation of regulations. MacArthur, fully aware of what was happening (including a raging bonfire), stayed in his bed.

The next morning, his subordinates waited for the commandant to erupt. Instead, he was quite pleased. "I could hardly resist the impulse to join them," he said to his adjutants. Red Blaik had made his first big impression on Douglas MacArthur.

Earl Henry "Red" Blaik was the son of a blacksmith, a Scottish Presbyterian who had emigrated from Glasgow. Like many sons of immigrants, Blaik gravitated to sports as his way of melting into the mainstream of American society. After playing football at Miami University of Ohio, he was heavily recruited by, and transferred to, West Point, where he played two more years and was a star baseball player.

After graduating, Blaik did a brief stint in the army as a cavalry officer, worked for his father, then bounced around in a series of coaching jobs. In 1939 and 1940, Army had suffered back-to-back losing seasons for the first time in 35 years and MacArthur—though heavily involved in the war effort—was at the forefront of a lobbying campaign to make Blaik the new head coach, and to change weight restrictions at West Point so that he could recruit larger linemen.

Blaik rewarded his mentor with back-to-back undefeated seasons. In 1944 and 1945 (when, it's important to point out, most college campuses were hurting for football players because of the war), Army went a combined 18–0 and won two national championships.

Blaik's success was built on the foundation he learned from MacArthur: supreme dedication, loyalty, toughness, discipline, and, above all else, a code of honor and secrecy. Not surprisingly, Blaik branded his Army football team with the name the Black Knights.

The Black Knights had a 32-game unbeaten streak from 1944 to 1947. Doc Blanchard won the Heisman Trophy at Army in 1945. Glenn Davis won it the following year. Both Blanchard and Davis were first-round picks, Blanchard in 1946 and Davis a year later. (Military obligations and injury would prevent both from having successful pro careers.)

But Blaik's real influence on football came from his ability to teach the men who taught the game. His nickname was "The Colonel." His style was tough and stern. And his motto was straight out of the old commandant himself: "Good fellows are a dime a dozen, but an aggressive leader is priceless."

And Vince Lombardi soaked up every word.

Vince Thomas Lombardi

In all, an unprecedented 20 coaches who stood on the sideline at West Point with Red Blaik would go on to become head coaches.

Army head coach Red Blaik was the mentor for scores of future head coaches, including Vince Lombardi.

Only one of them has his name carved on the side of the Super Bowl trophy.

Here's the background. If you don't know the story by now, you should. Lombardi is *La Storia* personified—the quintessential immigrant narrative of America in the 20th century. His grandparents came to America from Salerno in southern Italy. His father was a butcher. His mother, the daughter of a barber. He grew up in Sheepshead Bay, along the southern shank of Brooklyn, which faces the final stretches of the Atlantic Ocean before all those immigrant ships approached the mouth of New York Harbor and the Statue of Liberty.

Lombardi went to Fordham University on a football scholarship. He was not very big, only 5'8" and a shade less than 160 pounds.

But he played guard on the fabled Seven Blocks of Granite. Sleepy Jim Crowley, one of the Four Horsemen of Notre Dame in the 1920s, was his head coach. His position coach was Frank Leahy, who went on to become the head coach for the Irish many years later. So, Lombardi had the foundation of a real football pedigree when he graduated in 1937.

Across the Hudson River, Lombardi got his first job as an assistant coach at St. Cecilia in Englewood, New Jersey. After going back to Fordham, Lombardi accepted a job at West Point in 1949. Blaik was coming off another undefeated season. (Army was 8–0–1 in 1948.) Lombardi—a gruff, foul-mouthed Brooklynite who went to college in the Bronx and plied his bombastic personality into success in North Jersey—was about to become humbled by one of the greatest coaches of his time. Blaik was righteous—in the mold of Amos Alonzo Stagg and Walter Camp. The Colonel did not curse. Lombardi was in awe of him. "Vince's bluster turned to obsequiousness when he was within range of the coach," wrote Lombardi biographer David Maraniss. "At times, he came across like a boot-licking corporal…"

Lombardi recorded, analyzed, and committed to memory everything Blaik said and did. It was Blaik who introduced the two-platoon system, which MacArthur—even from his post in Tokyo as the Allied commander of the Japanese postwar recovery—watched and praised. Lombardi's role in the Blaik system was critical. And in 1949, Army went undefeated again, 9–0. But during Lombardi's five seasons at West Point, the national criticism of Blaik grew its loudest. The platoon system was viewed as heresy. And Blaik's high and mighty public persona was spoiled by whispers from Columbia to Stanford that the Army teams played dirty football.

All this made the Colonel all the more paranoid and his demand for loyalty unrelenting. Lombardi never wavered, and Blaik frequently rewarded him. In 1951, when MacArthur asked Blaik to send several of his coaches to Japan and Korea to teach football to local athletes, Lombardi headed the delegation.

These were heady times for Blaik and his prized assistants, including Lombardi. The team had just finished an 8–1 season in 1950, claiming the No. 2 spot in the national rankings. From 1944 to 1950, in only one season had Army failed to win eight games.

But it all came crashing down on the morning of August 3, 1951. The U.S. Military Academy, in its worst scandal to date, expelled 90 cadets for violating the honor code. In that expulsion, 60 varsity athletes were gone, including 37 members of Blaik's football team. His son, Bob, who was penciled in as the starting quarterback, was among those dismissed from West Point.

Shocked and embarrassed by the waves of negative publicity, Blaik closed ranks and dug in. Lombardi admired his resolve. It was at this point that his skepticism of the press hardened. Lombardi was learning a valuable lesson. Later, despite all his success— winning five NFL titles in seven years and the first two Super Bowls—Lombardi kept reporters at a distance. "The press can be, and often is, a horror for me," Lombardi said in 1967, at the height of his appeal and power.

Blaik soldiered on at Army for seven more seasons. But, in 1954, Lombardi took a job with the New York Giants. And the year after Blaik left West Point, after an 8–0 season, Lombardi became the head coach of the Green Bay Packers in 1959. From the moment Lombardi arrived in Wisconsin, it might as well have been Red Blaik barking on the sideline. In everything Lombardi said and did, you could hear the Colonel's words and voice.

The Packers—one of the league's founding and most successful teams—had fallen on hard times. So, just like MacArthur as the new West Point commandant, just like Blaik as the new Army head football coach, Lombardi's challenge was clear as could be. He was to bring the Packers back to glory. And like MacArthur and Blaik, Lombardi did it with an abrupt and radical break from the past.

"What a difference a year and a man can make," wrote Lee Remmel in the *Green Bay Press-Gazette*. Lombardi's training camp that summer was brutal. He was tough, demanding, and profane. Players jogged from drill to drill. And when practice was "over," that's when Lombardi presided over a series of wind sprints and gassers that had players heaving and vomiting as they walked back to the locker room.

His style backed up his words. "You don't win once in a while, you don't do things right once in a while," Lombardi warned his team. "Winning is a habit. Winning is not a sometime thing. It's an all-the-time thing. It has always been an American zeal to be first in anything we do, and to win, and to win, and to win."

Sounds like Blaik quoting MacArthur quoting Dewey. And that's what Lombardi did—win and win and win. The Packers won NFL championships in 1961, 1962, 1965, 1966, and 1967, and Lombardi became the only man to lead his team to titles in three straight seasons. And the Packers won Super Bowls I and II, restoring the nickname "Titletown" to the tiny city of Green Bay, making Lambeau Field a national cathedral of football and Lombardi the patron saint of American sports in the 1960s.

It is important to remember, too, that Lombardi accomplished what he did at the precise time when broadcast television fully embraced professional football. So, while what MacArthur and Blaik said and did were widely read and fully woven into the American cultural fabric, what Lombardi accomplished was being delivered by a far more powerful and pervasive medium. In America's living rooms, in living color (as they liked to say), here was Lombardi—the embodiment of the American immigrant dream—as a powerful symbol for the political rationalization of the game of football.

So he reached icon status. But his legacy runs deeper than that. Go back for a moment to St. Cecilia High School in Englewood, New Jersey—the place where Lombardi got his first job out of Fordham. At St. Cecilia's, Lombardi had to pull double duty to earn his pay, so he also coached the basketball team. His star player was a kid named Mickey Corcoran.

Ten years later, Mickey Corcoran was the first head basketball coach at River Dell High School in nearby Oradell, New Jersey. His star player was Bill Parcells.

Bill Parcells

As it happens, Duane Charles Parcells was born in Englewood, New Jersey, in 1941. His mother was Italian. His father, who was Irish, was an outstanding baseball player who went to Georgetown University and served for several years in the FBI. So, his son, who got the nickname Bill in grade school, had athletics and discipline introduced to his life before he met Mickey Corcoran at River Dell High School in 1959.

Corcoran was very tough on his star basketball player. Parcells, who was 6'2" and a ferocious competitor, led the team in scoring, but he had a mercurial temper—even as a teenager. "Don't be afraid to put a foot in his ass if you have to," Parcells's father once told Corcoran. Well, the coach never did that. But he knew he had to put his foot down.

"I was 15 years old and we were up by 17 and he took me out of the game because I got a technical foul and we got beat by one," said Parcells. Corcoran told him, "Parcells, you weren't worth the two points you cost us on that technical foul you drew and if you ever get another one, you ain't gonna play another minute here."

At River Dell High, Parcells also played quarterback on the football team. His coach was Tom Cahill, another tough taskmaster. After leaving River Dell, Cahill landed his first big job—as the head football coach at the U.S. Military Academy. He arrived in West Point in 1966, the year he hired a young linebacker who had just been cut by the Detroit Lions. His name was Bill Parcells.

Parcells spent three years under Cahill at West Point. The DNA chain from MacArthur through Blaik and Lombardi was now complete. At Army, Parcells said he learned important leadership lessons.

"It was being around other coaches there, watching and learning," Parcells said. "I was a younger coach on a more veteran staff. That helped reign in what would have been more impulsive decisions and forced me to be more analytical before I spoke or suggested things. But they liked my passion for the game and would chalk up my mistakes to being eager. They let me coach, and that was something that I always tried to let my coaches do."

But at West Point, Parcells learned something far more valuable, something that he would learn to lean on heavily once he got to the NFL.

"Loyalty was another aspect that was emphasized there to your staff members," said Parcells, who also served under Bob Knight as an assistant coach on the West Point basketball team. "I always tried to carry that with me."

Indeed, when the New York Giants hired Parcells as the head coach in 1983, they knew they were getting somebody who would instill discipline and toughness. "The hero and the coward feel the same pain," Parcells was fond of telling his players. "It's what they do next that separates them."

But Parcells—like Lombardi, Blaik, and MacArthur—demanded something more, something that would make him, and the Giants, a champion: unrelenting dedication and loyalty to the team, and the coach. You did not double-cross him.

Using a unique blend of charm, sarcasm, and Jersey-guy profanity, Parcells was a master motivator and psychologist. He molded the mercurial linebacker Lawrence Taylor into a human nightmare for opposing quarterbacks. He also pushed a reticent young Phil Simms to be a fiery leader and highly efficient quarterback.

Parcells hoisted his first Lombardi Trophy in 1986, giving the Giants their first NFL title in 30 years. Four years later, the Giants won Super Bowl XXV.

Bill Parcells brought the lessons he learned at West Point to the New York Giants in 1983.

Like MacArthur and Blaik and Lombardi (and Knight), Parcells was very suspicious of the press. (Remember, reporters, he said, were Communists, subversives from within.) He liked to joust with reporters, but that was only a form of putdown. He rarely let one into his inner circle. Vinny DiTrani of the *Bergen Record* is one. Mike Francesca of WFAN radio is another. I had a brief star turn into the inner sanctum, but I lost his trust on draft day in 1997.

At the time, Parcells was head coach of the Giants' crosstown rivals, the New York Jets—again, trying to teach his approach to life and football to a team that had been a train wreck for nearly a generation. Parcells had the first pick in the draft but had traded down, and I was embedded in the team's locker room for ESPN's live coverage. One of the juicier subjects on my plate was the fact that one of Parcells's favorite players, wide receiver Keyshawn Johnson, had just written a book called *Just Give Me the Damn Ball*, in which he skewered quarterback Neil O'Donnell as a "stiff puppet," and the diminutive wide receiver Wayne Chrebet as a "team mascot."

Parcells was mum on the book. The implication was that he was happy that Johnson had shaken things up. (They remain friends to this day.) The day before the draft, I had suggested to the team's public relations director at the time, Frank Ramos, that I would leave the subject alone. I never should have done that, because the next day, our draft coverage included a rather rancid live debate on the subject—right before Chris Berman tossed to me in the Jets locker room! I had no choice. I had to ask Parcells about the book.

My rationale was based on his own thinking. Here was Johnson, engaging in the ultimate act of disloyalty toward two teammates. Fair game, I thought. After all, Parcells wrote the following words in his own book of advice for businessmen: "The first task of leadership is to promote—and enforce—collective loyalty.... Disunity will kill you quick. One maverick can capsize a ship."

I thought that by asking him about Johnson, I could get him to talk about the essence of what he preaches as a head coach. What I didn't realize at the time was that if he had responded to me, Parcells would be just as guilty as Johnson. Any criticism of Johnson could be interpreted as an act of disloyalty toward the team. Me? I was just another Communist. I didn't count. Only Johnson and the team mattered.

So, after Berman tossed to me, Parcells and I briefly discussed his early draft picks. Then I asked a question about Johnson's book. Despite my earlier promise that I wouldn't, I think he would have looked past that one question. But when he refused to comment, I went too far, asking not one, but two follow-up questions. No comment, and no comment. I tossed it back to Berman in New York. And within seconds Parcells threw me out of the locker room—soundtrack provided by his full-throated profanity.

After that incident, Parcells did not speak to me, or look at me, for years. He had showed me kindness and given me help, and I had crossed him. Simply put, I had been disloyal. Nevertheless, on the day he left the Jets, as he walked past Ramos's office, Parcells grabbed my arm and said, "The war is over, Sal. The war is over."

The way he handles the press is right out of the West Point playbook. The signature move: secrecy. He refused to allow his assistant coaches to talk to reporters. He did not want strategy or injuries leaked to the papers. So his teams always spoke with one voice.

No one was better in carrying out that mandate than the son of a Naval Academy coach who Parcells made the Giants' defensive coordinator in 1983, with a special emphasis on linebackers. His name was Bill Belichick.

Bill Belichick

If, as David Halberstam once wrote, Parcells was "the lineal descendant of Vince Lombardi," then Bill Belichick was a natural heir.

A brilliant tactician and designer from the outset, Belichick's specialty was linebackers, the fulcrum of what Parcells expected his defense to do—stop the running game, torment the quarterback (not necessarily in that order). Parcells's game was always about finding ways to extract superior field position. He wanted his opposition to go farther and fight harder for yardage. This gave him a tactical advantage, more choices in his play calling, and more stamina for his team. He admitted it was a concept forged at West Point.

"I do believe that football is and will forever be a field position game," Parcells said. "Certain areas of the field command a certain limited-risk play-selection strategy. That has served me well over the years. The West Coast gurus don't and never will understand that. [They] just run their plays."

To Parcells, Belichick brought with him a military pedigree. He did not serve in the armed forces. But his father, Steve, coached at the Naval Academy for 33 years. And he was very smart, attending the prestigious Phillips Academy at Andover and Wesleyan University, where he got a degree in economics.

Within the Parcells Big Blue regime, Belichick was the first lieutenant, implementing that field position strategy in a way that was unprecedented. The Giants did not have a "system" of defense. Belichick's philosophy was that—game-by-game—he would design a defense that found an offense's strength and took it away, and then found its weakness and exploited it.

Sounds simple enough, but it requires practically reinventing your defense each week, which requires an extraordinary amount of film study of the opposition's players, tendencies, and play calling in certain situations. Belichick was always looking for any edge, any way to get an advantage.

And that required another tenet of the Parcells's methodology that had been influenced by his West Point roots: secrecy. Build a wall around your team. Why? When you're redesigning your defense week by week, it's imperative nobody knows what's going on.

"Little Bill is like Big Bill in that regard," said a defensive end who played for both. "If you talk, you get fined. Eventually, you will be gone. It won't be tolerated. Players they bring in understand that. You cannot violate that." It's like *omerta*, the code of silence of La Cosa Nostra. But the business here is championship football.

Belichick brought this single-minded focus to his first head coaching job in Cleveland in 1991. But it was not a good fit. While Parcells can often disarm with the Irish-Italian charm he learned from his parents, in the shadow of living in the big city, Belichick is cold and aloof. His nickname was "Doom." In Cleveland, Belichick forgot that, more than being the lead tactician, the head coach of an NFL team is the CEO and spokesman for a franchise, for a city. What he says, how he acts when the cameras are rolling, is how the public will perceive him—and thus the team itself. But Belichick could not hide his contempt for reporters—once bringing the beat writer for the *The Plain Dealer* to near tears in 1994. Belichick lasted just five years—after his last season the Browns were moved to Baltimore and renamed the Ravens.

Belichick followed Parcells to the Patriots, then the Jets, then broke away from his mentor to become the head coach in New England in 2000. His methods refined, Belichick found the right mix of front office talent and players to finally evolve into a successful head coach. With a former small-college football player named Scott Pioli (who would later marry Parcells's daughter, Dallas) scouting and helping to select players, and Tom Brady emerging as a true superstar at quarterback, the Patriots under Belichick proved to be a natural successor to the MacArthur-Blaik-Lombardi-Parcells heritage.

In 2001, the Patriots won their first of three Super Bowls in four years, establishing Belichick as the top coach of his generation. He is one of only nine coaches in history with three or more NFL titles, creating pro football's first dynasty of the 21st century.

In the last two years of that run, one of his most trusted adjutants was a guy Belichick hired right out of college to make copies in the press room back in Cleveland. His name: Eric Mangini.

Eric Mangini

On September 9, 2007, Eric Mangini did the unthinkable in the MacArthur-Blaik-Lombardi-Parcells-Belichick chain of custody of the West Point tradition. He broke the code of silence. Mangini talked. He named names.

Let's rewind for a second. In Cleveland, in 1994, Belichick hired Mangini, who also went to Wesleyan. Played fullback. They were in the same fraternity, Chi Psi. With the Browns, at age 23, Mangini started as a ball boy. Then, he worked as copy runner in the press box, then coaching assistant, splicing film study together for the other coaches. This was the way Belichick learned from his father at the Naval Academy, watching from the ground up, cutting film, fetching coffee.

In Mangini, Belichick saw the same protégé Parcells saw. And Corcoran developed. And Lombardi nurtured. And Blaik brought on board. And MacArthur discovered.

Mangini took it all in—how to game plan, how to design defense, how to handle players, how to deal with the press. All from Belichick. So, Mangini didn't understand Belichick's objection when he left New England to coach the Jets, and he certainly didn't understand Belichick recoiling at the fact that the Jets were interested in some of New England's players. Isn't this what Belichick had taught him, what had been handed down from the West Point tree—to win at all costs?

But their relationship was frozen in a paranoid state of mutual distrust. And on September 9, on the opening day of the 2007 season, midway through the Patriots beatdown of the Jets, Mangini was notified that one of Belichick's video assistants, Matt Estrella, was credentialed, standing on the Patriots sideline, illegally taping the Jets' defensive coaching staff—trying to steal New York's signals.

What made this so galling is that NFL commissioner Roger Goodell had just sent all 32 teams a letter, reinforcing the league's rules against videotaping the opposing sideline. Estrella's credentials were pulled. His camera was confiscated by NFL security.

Simply put, Mangini had turned in his former boss.

Some called him a whistleblower. Others in the Parcells-Belichick sphere whispered that Mangini—the good son, the Coach of the Year in the AFC in 2006, the handpicked chairman of Football America—was a snitch. The code of silence had been broken.

Goodell investigated and brought immediate punishment—Belichick was fined $500,000. The team was fined another $250,000 and forfeited a first-round draft pick. But it was not that easy. Spygate, as it was dubbed by the *New York Daily News*, left a seemingly indelible scarlet "S" on the Patriots pursuit of a perfect season.

———

And, on the eve of the Thanksgiving Day showdown with the Cowboys, Mangini was looking for a way out—any way out—of a season that had turned into a nightmare.

On The FAN, the word "Mangenius" was no longer a moniker of radio respect. Instead, from Levittown to Lodi, it was delivered with a large gulp of sarcasm. And driving to work, Woody Johnson could hear it, wondering how it all came unraveled so quickly. The arc of the Jets' revival was not supposed to go like this.

On Thanksgiving Day, there was no way out. Just more horror. A national television audience watched the Dallas Cowboys wallpaper the New York Jets 34–3.

6

"All warfare is based on deception."

—Sun Tzu

How Football Explains
the Battle of Midway

Tom Brady had no idea where they were coming from.

Of course, we should have all seen this coming, right? A week earlier, on a Sunday night, with Al Michaels and John Madden aghast on NBC's *Football Night in America*, the Philadelphia Eagles battered Brady, rope-tied Randy Moss, and nearly took home the grand prize of the 2007 NFL season: beating the heretofore perfect Patriots. But Brady had pulled out another win, and here he was eight days later—again on national television—getting hit in the mouth by Ray Lewis, slapped around by Haloti Ngata, and chased by Terrell Suggs, while a ruinous wind from the Chesapeake Bay whipped through M&T Bank Stadium, where a constant swirl of candy wrappers, paper cups, and snow decorated the coldest early December night in Baltimore in more than a generation.

On the Baltimore sideline, defensive coordinator Rex Ryan—the eldest son of that mad quarterback killer, Buddy, who put together the meanest defense in Super Bowl history with the Chicago Bears in 1985—was running up and down the field, berating officials, screaming instructions, flailing his arms with last-minute signals so that Brady did, indeed, have no idea where they—the ravenous Ravens—were coming from.

"They simply did stuff we'd never seen before," Brady would confide after the game.

Never seen before?! C'mon, a Bill Belichick team unprepared? Well, it sure looked that way. Ryan had succeeded in deceiving the master of deception himself. Evidently, nobody saw this coming—not Tony, Jaws, and Mike in the *Monday Night Football* booth, not the Vegas odds makers (the Ravens were three-touchdown underdogs), and certainly not the quarterback with the three Super Bowl rings.

Now, with just 1:48 remaining in the fourth quarter, and the sold-out purple-and-black crowd smelling a huge upset, screaming, chanting, banging their chairs to a ear-splitting pitch, Brady walked up to the line of scrimmage at the Ravens' 30-yard line, down by four points—trailing this late in a game for the first time all season.

All New England needed was one yard to get a first down, to keep the drive going, to keep the story of an undefeated season alive for another set of downs. This is the drama that Walter Camp and Amos Alonzo Stagg had always hoped for: the quarterback at the helm, the field to be conquered, the defense trying to hold its ground, the territory at stake—the crowd engaged to the point of delirium. Of course, the granddads of American football could never have imagined that at that very moment, the audience at home, watching on TV, would be in the millions—in fact, the largest to watch a *Monday Night Football* game all season.

Center Dan Koppen snapped the football to Brady. Brady handed it to fullback Heath Evans, who was stopped stone-cold for a one-yard loss by a gang of Ravens led by Ngata, who is the size of a rhino and who moves like a panther and who was given the regal full name of Etuini Haloti Ngata by his mother, Olga, who was born on the tiny island of Tonga in the South Pacific. In Tongan, Ngata means "the end"—the end of the road, the line, anything. But Ngata's tackle was a false stop.

Before the snap, before Ngata pounced on Evans, a referee's whistle had been drowned out by the crowd, which was sounding more and more like an F-14 taking off in your ear. The officials had blown the play dead. Backup guard Russ Hochstein, who was on the field only because starter Stephen Neal was injured, had jumped out of his stance. The false start penalty, normally a drive killer, had set the Patriots back five yards, but it reset the drama, giving Brady one more play to keep the perfect season alive.

Patriots quarterback Tom Brady calmly points out defenders during New England's 27–24 comeback victory against the Ravens in 2007.

And Brady had no idea where they would be coming from. He approached the line of scrimmage, and Ray Lewis and his running mate, linebacker Bart Scott, and the two safeties, Ed Reed and Dawan Landry, were darting in and out and side to side, and on the sideline, Rex Ryan, who looked like "Doc" in the movie *Back to the Future*, a disheveled, but highly competent, mess. There was no way to tell where the blitz was coming from, but it was coming, that much was sure.

In the shotgun formation, about six yards behind Koppen, Brady stepped into the breach and looked out onto the field and he knew, right from the beginning, this would be on him. It was now fourth down, six yards to go to keep this unbeaten streak alive for another set of downs. That's all Brady wanted. There was no guarantee New England would score. The Patriots just needed to capture six more yards, hold it, and keep advancing— the essence of the game. There has been only one book written about Tom Brady. It's aptly called *Moving the Chains*, referring to that perfect little concept set down by the founders of the game in 1882, when they created the first down. Keep moving the chains, keep capturing territory, keep the narrative of the game going, keep the fans engaged.

But, in the modern design of the game, that's not as easy as it sounds, because week in and week out, defensive coordinators are trying to decapitate the offense—yes, cut its head off by knocking out the quarterback. That's the name of the game, now. It was always that way, really, with defensive end Deacon Jones rapping his giant, padded paws across the helmet ear hole of offensive linemen—ah, the head slap—which itself was later outlawed. But Jones actually named this violent little statistical category pro football now lives by, called "the sack," which was perfected inhumanely by Lawrence Taylor, the Parcells-Belichick creation who had a toxic brew of anger and skill and who is captured by

NFL Films screaming, "Let's run around like a bunch of crazed dogs!" Jones and Taylor were the godfathers of the sack 25 years ago. Now, it is the very essence of the game. And you can blame Bill Belichick for that, too.

In the 2003 AFC Championship Game, played at snowy Gillette Stadium in Foxborough, Massachusetts, the Patriots secondary—Belichick's specialty—had strict instructions to do everything within the rules, and whatever they could get away with, to disrupt, harass, hold, and punish the polished wide receivers of the Indianapolis Colts. Pro Bowl wide receiver Marvin Harrison was kept out of the end zone. Peyton Manning was intercepted four times. And the Patriots went to the Super Bowl.

And Colts team president Bill Polian pitched a fit. The following spring, Polian's complaints were brought to a meeting of the owners, general managers, and coaches at the Breaker's Hotel in Palm Beach, Florida. With the ocean crashing outside, and their wives and kids playing in the sun by the pool, and about two dozen reporters mingling in the lobby designed to host the rich and famous, the NFL's vice president of officiating, Mike Pereira, was in a room with the shades drawn all the way down and a video projector, showing play after play in the AFC Championship Game where Patriots cornerback Ty Law was grabbing, clutching, and holding Harrison—while the referees kept their yellow flags in their pockets. League rules state that a defender cannot touch a wide receiver five yards beyond the line of scrimmage. It's called the five-yard no-chuck rule. But it wasn't being called. In the future, promised Pereira, it would be.

And the future is now. Now, wide receivers run free after five yards, or those yellow flags quickly fly. As a result, scoring has been up. So, that means the only way to attack the passing game, which is the essence of pro football, is to attack it at the point of attack, namely the guy dropping back to throw the football. And the only way to accomplish that is *not* to let him know where you're coming from.

So, if you are Tom Brady, and you have fourth-and-six and your undefeated season is teetering on extinction, you have to try to figure that out. And, if you are his head coach, you have to give Brady any possible edge. Study tendencies. Pay close attention to the defensive personnel shuttling on and off the field. Look at the defensive alignment when you approach the line of scrimmage. Before you snap the ball, you've got to figure out where they are coming from.

But, sometimes, a defense is too good at disguising that. So, you can't be afraid to go further. Go to the source: the defensive coordinator. You've got to figure out what the defensive coordinator is doing on the sideline, what defense he is calling. You've got to study his signals, try to decode them.

Yes, let's call it what it is: you've got to try to steal the signs. Don't be squeamish about it. It's the American way. How do you think America won World War II?

———

You always hear football players talk about "going to war" on Sunday. "These are the guys I go to war with," is a common way of describing the bond that players often try to form with one another.

And common football terms and tactics come right from the combat lexicon. "Blitz" the quarterback. The quarterback throws "a bomb." The San Francisco 49ers own a prolific "aerial attack." Randy Moss is the "tip of the spear" for the Patriots offense.

But equating football to actual combat is an affront to anybody who has ever served in uniform.

Of course, football is a violent game. It has, on rare occasions, resulted in death. But nobody is shooting real bullets at you—

nobody is walking up to you in a crowded market in Baghdad with a flak jacket full of C-4 and ball-bearings and pressing a button that ends your life.

"In football," said sociologist Harry Edwards, "you have a sport which is as close as you can get to war and still stay civil. But football and war are nowhere close. It's the difference between having a serious concussion and having your head blown off."

So, it's important to be careful when attempting to use war as a metaphor for football. The result is often hackneyed clichés that sound trite and out of place. But there is one area where American football, because of how the game grew to be sophisticated and complex, mirrors one aspect of what often happens between two parties at war: espionage. In war and in football, it is critically important to gather intelligence about the enemy.

Sun Tzu said so around 400 B.C. In his widely quoted treatises called *The Art of War*, Sun Tzu called one chapter "The Employment of Secret Agents." He writes in subheading No. 4: "What is called foreknowledge cannot be elicited from spirits, nor from gods, nor by analogy with past events, nor from calculations. It must be obtained from the men who know the enemy situation."

In short, the best intelligence is human intelligence. Why? Because in any form of conflict between two parties, it's critical that the tactics be concealed. "A skilled general must be master of the complementary arts of simulation and dissimulation; while creating shapes to confuse and delude the enemy, he conceals his true dispositions and ultimate intent...the victorious situation [is the] product of his creative imagination," wrote Sun Tzu. (Tom Brady had no idea where they were coming from!)

Prior to the events of 9/11, what was considered the most lethal and effective surprise attack perpetrated against the United States? The Japanese destruction of the American fleet at Pearl Harbor on December 7, 1941.

At the time, Japan had the largest fleet and the best-trained sailors and carrier-based pilots in the world. And after the spectacular victory in Hawaii, the Imperial fleet claimed Guam and was determined to deliver a knockout blow to the bewildered American fleet at the island of Midway, the so-called sentry to Hawaii.

The plan was to cut off the Americans at Midway, then circle back west to take Fiji and bomb Australia into an early surrender, then return to the Hawaiian Islands for the final blow against the United States—all before August of 1942.

But a guy in his bathrobe and slippers put a stop to it all.

Yes, the Japanese had superior naval forces at the time. But Admiral Isoroku Yamamoto, the architect of the sneak attack at Pearl Harbor, also had something far more lethal at his disposal, a naval code called JN-25. At the time, it was considered the most sophisticated military code in the world, consisting of more than 45,000 five-digit numbers. To use a football metaphor, the U.S. Navy needed to steal Japan's signs. America was in the process of rebuilding its fleet. The Japanese were about to embark on their ambitious plan in the South Pacific. Time was of essence.

But Admiral Chester W. Nimitz, commander of allied naval forces in the Pacific, had a secret weapon. His name was Commander Joseph J. Rochefort, a Naval Academy graduate who was fluent in Japanese and a brilliant mathematician. "He wore his hair in the 'mad-professor' style and talked disjointedly because his mouth could not keep up with his mind," wrote D. van der Vat in his groundbreaking history of World War II in the Pacific, *The Pacific Campaign*. "His forte was pure mathematics...his mind unfettered by orthodox officer training."

This iconoclast was in charge of something called the Pacific Fleet Combat Intelligence Unit (known as HYPO), a group of cryptanalysts who were relegated to a windowless basement office on the navy base at Pearl Harbor. Often shunned and misunderstood, Rochefort and his team worked long hours poring over Japanese transmissions, trying to crack JN-25. Lacking sleep and often refusing to eat, Rochefort walked around his bivouac in his bathrobe and slippers, mumbling to himself.

But in the spring of 1942, Rochefort and his team solved the code. He tested it by sending a decoy message, transmitted over a clear channel so the Japanese would easily intercept it—that Midway Island was lacking adequate water supplies. The Japanese bought it, revealing their plan: an attack on Midway in mid-June.

The United States Navy defeated the Japanese in the Battle of Midway in 1942, partly thanks to codes intercepted before the enemy had been engaged.

If they had not known the Japanese were coming, the American forces faced certain annihilation. When he embarked on the attack on Midway, Yamamoto sailed with an armada of more than 200 ships. Nearly 100,000 sailors and pilots—and an astonishing 20 admirals—were under his command. This battle group included four powerful aircraft carriers, *Akagi, Kaga, Hiryu,* and *Soryu*—the finest in the world at the time.

In short, Nimitz was badly outnumbered. But Yamamoto was outcoached. The American carriers—*Hornet, Enterprise,* and *Yorktown,* which recently had been rebuilt in Pearl Harbor—knew exactly where the Japanese were coming from—thanks to Commander Rochefort and his unorthodox gang of code breakers.

Using their newly refurbished SBD Dauntless carrier-based dive-bombers, the American fleet destroyed squadrons of Japanese planes while they were fueling and loading ordnance on the carrier decks. Within minutes on the morning of June 4, 1942, three of the Japanese carriers were sunk—gone. Yamamoto never got near Midway. And the tide was turned for good in the Pacific.

Midway was the first decisive naval defeat of the Japanese in more than three centuries. It effectively ended the Japanese hegemony in the Pacific and gave America time to rebuild its fleet and plan and execute a three-year-long campaign of island hopping that eventually led to General Douglas MacArthur accepting the Japanese surrender on the carrier *Yorktown* in 1945.

———————

Remember Paul D. Hubbard, the quarterback on the deaf football team at Gallaudet University? He invented the huddle to stop the opposition from stealing his American Sign Language signals to his offensive teammates. That was 1894.

Exactly one hundred years later, the NFL figured out how to really solve Paul Hubbard's problem. In 1994, the NFL finally allowed radio communication between a coach on the sideline and the quarterback on the field.

The minutes from the 1994 league meeting that approved the electronic communication state that the new system "replace and improve upon the current procedure of hand-signaling" providing "signals secure from eavesdropping and other observations" that often resulted in the stealing of signs.

As one member of the committee remarked: "This solves a problem of somewhat primitive communication we've had for decades. Now, a coach and quarterback can better communicate in secret."

Coaches covering their mouths while calling plays from the sideline has become an accepted practice in today's game.

The minutes make it clear that, after weeks of debate and two years of tests, secrecy was the ultimate goal. "The message sent from the sideline coach's radio will be encrypted ('scrambled') for security," the minutes state. "The receiving device in the quarterback's helmet will instantaneously decode the scrambled message for him. The encryption scheme will have more than 268 million possible codes, and each team will have its own, indecipherable by any other team or person attempting to listen."

But in something right out of Commander Rochefort's cryptanalyst playbook, teams were immediately accused of fooling with the assigned radio frequencies or the encryption equipment. No longer able to steal the offensive signals, coaches were trying to intercept them—or, at best, interrupt them.

In 1996, a visiting quarterback complained that as he looked toward the sideline and waited for the coach to talk to him about the next play, he heard someone say in his helmet, "Need a cart of Polish dogs in section 114."

There were back-channel whispers that several teams, most notably the Cowboys under Jimmy Johnson, the Patriots under Bill Parcells, and the Steelers under Bill Cowher, routinely jammed the coach-to-quarterback radio signals, especially at critical moments in a game.

And coaches are still concerned about lipreading. When you see Mike Holmgren or Andy Reid covering their lips with large white laminated play cards as they talk to their quarterbacks on the field, that's because they don't want the coaches on the opposite sideline, or scouts using binoculars in the press box, to read their lips—and then match the verbiage to the play called. Intercepting the play this way may not have immediate benefit. But it could be used in halftime adjustments or when the two teams meet again.

And there are concerns that jamming the coach-to-quarterback signals is still attempted. Guess who draws some of the greatest suspicion? The New England Patriots. When the Jacksonville Jaguars went to Foxborough on January 12, 2008, to play the Patriots in a divisional round playoff game at Gillette Stadium, Jags head coach Jack Del Rio brought extra technical personnel to make sure there were no attempts at jamming radio communication to Jacksonville quarterback David Garrard. "Everybody knows that it happens all the time at Gillette—the comms just go down," said one league official who asked not to be identified. "So, Jack was just playing it safe." There were no incidents of jamming during the game, but the threat was certainly enough to give Del Rio something else to think about and plan for.

—·—

While the coach-to-quarterback communication gear was designed to modernize offensive play calling and make it more secure, there is still no such system in place for defensive coaches. It's still a primitive set of hand and arm signals.

"And we've been trying to steal them for decades," said former quarterback Ron Jaworski. "There is an old saying in the NFL: if you ain't cheatin', you ain't tryin'."

Two days before Super Bowl XLII, NFL commissioner Roger Goodell said, "I'm not sure that there is a coach in the league that doesn't expect that their signals are being intercepted by opposing teams."

Goodell went further: it was up to the teams to conceal what they are doing, not up to the opposition to stop trying to steal signs. Espionage, Goodell was acknowledging, is a time-honored tradition in American football.

At Super Bowl XLII, the suspicion of possible espionage was so high that both teams had their practice facilities surrounded by a phalanx of police officers supplied by the City of Phoenix, supervised by a team of NFL security officers imported from all 32 teams. But the level of paranoia was so acute that none of the NFL security personnel from any NFC East team could be deployed at the Patriots facility. And none from the AFC East teams could monitor suspicious activity at the Giants facility. Giants head coach Tom Coughlin was taking no chances. According to two Giants team officials, the Patriots were caught taping a defensive assistant giving signals during a preseason game in 2006. The Giants did not turn Belichick in, a league source said.

Belichick has long been suspicious of reporters giving away his secrets, too—not only in writing or broadcasting the information, but in sidebar conversations with coaches and players from other teams. He has a right to mistrust some of them. Some of the better-known national reporters often go on drinking binges with their buddies in the NFL coaching fraternity. Their habits and friends are well known and monitored by members of the public relations staffs, who often warn their coaches of this kind of suspicious activity.

At the Super Bowl in Arizona, Belichick took no chances. The buses arriving daily with reporters for the NFL-sponsored press availabilities were diverted around the back of the hotel housing the Patriots in North Scottsdale. No reporter was allowed to hang out in the lobby. (I was thrown out of the Patriots' hotel lobby the day before Super Bowl XLII.)

This was all brought on by Spygate. When Belichick and the Patriots were punished for spying on the Jets, they had stepped over the line from the accepted forms of espionage to a practice banned by the NFL: using videotaping equipment during the game to tape the opposition's sideline. While all is fair in love and war, football has some rules regarding the gathering of intelligence.

The NFL's Game Operations Manual reads, "No video recording devices of any kind are permitted to be in use in the coaches' booth, on the field, or in the locker room during the game."

But the Patriots under Belichick have been suspected of violating the rule for years. The Green Bay Packers claim that they stopped a Patriots video assistant—the same one caught by the Jets—from trying to videotape their sideline in 2006. At the league's annual meeting in the spring of 2007, the competition committee discussed several complaints that there were routine violations of the rule—not only by the Patriots.

Why tape the sideline? Videotaping is a much more effective way of stealing the signals of the defensive coaches. Once the signs are on tape, coaching assistants would play and replay the signals and then match them against the defense alignment or tactic called. This would give the offense an idea, for example, of where the blitz was coming from.

The suspicions were that Brady, more than any other quarterback, was benefiting from this illegal system. There has never been any proof, but there were strong suspicions that Belichick's trusted video guru, Ernie Adams, specialized in this kind of espionage: taking the videotape of the defensive signals, decoding them, and determining what defenses were called and could be called against Tom Brady and the Patriots offense. So, Goodell sent a strongly worded warning to each team reminding them of the rules.

"Videotaping of any type, including but not limited to taping of an opponent's offensive or defensive signals, is prohibited on the sidelines," Goodell wrote.

That letter was sent just prior to the start of the 2007 season. And it was in the first week of that season, at Giants Stadium, just 12 miles from the Park Avenue offices of the NFL, that Belichick was found guilty of videotaping the Jets' sideline.

After levying the fine against Belichick and the Patriots, Goodell concluded: "This episode represents a calculated and deliberate attempt to avoid longstanding rules designed to encourage fair play and promote honest competition on the playing field."

Goodell confiscated notes and videotapes dating back seven years. Indeed, during a meeting with the commissioner, Belichick suggested that the Patriots had been engaged in this illegal espionage since 2000, or throughout their unprecedented run of three Super Bowl titles in seven seasons. Were those titles tainted? Goodell, saying he did not want the material to fall into the wrong hands, destroyed the notes and the tapes, claiming that the benefit to the Patriots was minimal. If that's the case, why did they do it? The answer is obvious: they wanted to know where the blitz was coming from.

———

By the time Monday night, December 3, 2007, arrived and the thought of the Patriots—at that point 11–0—going undefeated had rolled itself through the American football consciousness, Rex Ryan was ready: nobody was stealing his signals. If Rex Ryan showed up at your front door, you'd think he was their to fix your cable hook-up—that's what he looks like, the guy next door you'd want playing right field in your Sunday morning beer league. But with his father, Buddy, and his brother, Rob, the Ryan family has coached in six Super Bowls, collecting three championships. Their legacy? The "46 defense" Buddy Ryan invented when he was with the 1985 Chicago Bears.

The '85 Bears—considered by many to be the greatest Super Bowl team ever—were coached by the irascible Mike Ditka, whose psychological equal happened to be Buddy Ryan, a straight-talkin' horse farmer from Oklahoma—one of those classic "it-ain't-braggin'-if'n-you-can-back-it-up" guys.

In 1985, Buddy backed it up. With Ditka the fiery head man, Ryan took care of the defense, which made a mockery of the playoffs after going 15–1 that year. In the postseason, the Bears won three games by a combined 91–10, the greatest postseason margin of victory in the Super Bowl era. Without breaking a sweat, they shut out the New York Giants and Los Angeles Rams by a combined 45–0 to reach Super Bowl XX. In that game, the New England Patriots managed just seven yards on 11 rushing attempts—seven yards all game! And their starting quarterback, Tony Eason, was benched before he completed a pass—and before he got his head taken off by Ryan's relentless defense. In a nice piece of coincidence, the Bears scored 46 points to beat the Patriots in what was the most lopsided (46–10) Super Bowl win to date. And Ryan was carried off the field—the first time a defensive coordinator had been given such an honor after the Super Bowl.

With two future Hall of Famers—defensive lineman Dan Hampton and middle linebacker Mike Singletary ("Hey, baby, I'm gonna be here all day, baby. I like this kind of party. I like this kind of party, baby!")—Ryan's defense had one goal that subordinated all others: get to the quarterback at all costs. The name "46" comes not from a defensive alignment, but from the number worn by former Bears safety Doug Plank, one of Ryan's favorites. Bringing the hard-hitting Plank down to the line of scrimmage, Ryan wanted to create extra pressure by isolating the offensive linemen one-on-one in a way that prevented them from getting any help. Then it was up to the defensive players to whip their man in those one-on-one match-ups, which they frequently did.

Listen to the names of Ryan's defensive calls out of the 46. "Lightning"—designed to drive an electric shock of fear through the quarterback's heart. "Thunder"—make the QB physically ill from the sight of a never-ending toxic variation of blitzes from every possible angle. "Maniac"—give the quarterback just one thought: *Am I going to physically survive this football game?*

That brand of football was branded into the horse farmer's two boys, who grew up knowing that they would do one thing: coach defensive football at the highest level. And in 2006, the Ravens defense under Rex Ryan finished first in the NFL.

So, full of Ryan family bluster, the Ravens entered the Monday night game with the Patriots believing that they were going to maul Brady and stop the Patriots' winning streak. There would be no 12–0, despite what they were saying on ESPN or out in Vegas.

And Ryan was adamant, too, that even though the Patriots were on their way to setting the single-season record for points scored, there would be no gimmicks. No decoys on the sideline to try to hide the signals, as head coach Brian Billick had implored—in fact, instructed—him to do. No, this was going to be the straight 46, a furious assault on the manhood of America's glamour boy quarterback.

But with 1:48 left, and the Ravens up by four, and Brady staring at a fourth down with six yards to go, Ryan did not call a blitz. Brady couldn't believe what he saw. The safeties were more than 20 yards off the line of scrimmage. Ray Lewis was seven yards deep—he wasn't coming. Brady didn't need to know what Rex Ryan had signaled in. He could see it. The Ravens were going to drop eight into coverage.

Brady was in the shotgun. He sent running back Kevin Faulk, who is money on critical downs, into the left flat. Linebacker Bart Scott crossed the entire line of scrimmage to follow him. Lewis was supposed to be the unblocked defender, watching Brady, who never takes off. So, the two future Hall of Famers played a little cat-and-mouse. Brady drifted his eyes toward Faulk, and Lewis followed him. But Lewis followed Brady's look just a moment too long, a few yards too much, leaving a huge hole. Brady quickly occupied it. He raced passed the line of scrimmage. Lewis tried to reverse himself, but his momentum had carried him too far, and Brady slid for a

12-yard gain, enough to move the chains. No blitz, no problem. First down, Patriots.

Five plays later, out of the corner of his eye, Brady saw wide receiver Jabbar Gaffney slicing into the left deep corner of the end zone. With a flick of his forearm, Brady threw the ball across his body—right to left. In a flash, the pass cut through the cold night air and found the streaking Gaffney, who grabbed it about shoulder high and tiptoed the final two steps to stay in bounds, collecting an eight-yard touchdown pass, the winning score.

Patriots 27, Baltimore 24. Perfection, though tainted, was preserved.

7

"The father is always a Republican toward his son."

—Robert Frost

How Football Explains
Father Knows Best

Tom Coughlin knew what he wanted to do—he wanted to do what he had always done, what he learned from his father, Lou, a tough Irishman, an ordnance demolition specialist in World War II—a veteran, too, of one unforgiving winter after another in remote upstate New York. The son could almost hear his father's voice: "You work through it. You work hard. You don't let up."

But, after 36 years of coaching at the collegiate and professional level, this was supposed to be the new Tom Coughlin—the kinder, gentler coach who agreed to assemble a weekly player's council for the redress of grievances, who promised to eliminate the sideline tirades that looked like he was about to pop a capillary at the sight of every missed tackle or questionable call, who would defy the nicknames that had branded him throughout his career: "The Tyrant," "Colonel Tom," and "Soup Nazi," a reference to the cartoonish *Seinfeld* character who suffers no fools in serving his precious soup.

Judy Coughlin pulled her husband aside. "Tom," she told him late in the 2006 season, "the media doesn't just dislike you, they hate you. They hate you. So I'm telling you right now, do something to help yourself." But this wasn't the first time Coughlin had been warned—by his friends or his family.

The evolution of Coughlin the disciplinarian had gone through one three-year tenure with the Giants when Bill Parcells was head coach. Coaching the wide receivers, Coughlin's tough love was exactly what Parcells was looking for. They won a Super Bowl together in 1990. Coughlin left the pros to be the head coach at Boston College, where his dictatorial style found no dissent. He then was hired as the original head coach of the Jaguars. In Jacksonville for eight years, Coughlin brought the team to the brink of the Super Bowl, but then his act quickly wore thin. He sparred with the media and his players, who snickered behind his back about his silly rules.

In 2002, he was fired, and spent two years trying to find another job. After missing the playoffs under Jim Fassel, who had gone to the Super Bowl but then lost his locker room by allowing some of his star players to yap too much to the press, the Giants were looking for somebody to clean house. Enter Colonel Coughlin, who brought his new rules with him: if a player showed up to a meeting on time, they were fined because they had not arrived five minutes early. Players were fined, too, for not having both feet on the floor during film sessions. He barked and growled, becoming a caricature of the whole business of pro football being run by obsessive egomaniacs who wanted total control over every aspect of the organization.

Now, the Giants were looking for something else, or Coughlin was in jeopardy of losing his job. The 2006 season ended with a first-round exit from the playoffs. Team ownership had rewarded him with a one-year raise, which amounted to a one-year audition. Change, or else. John Mara, who took over daily operations from his late father, team patriarch Wellington, ordered Coughlin to meet with each member of the New York media that wrote about the team on a daily basis. There was Ralph Vacchiano and Gary Myers of the *New York Daily News*, John Branch of *The New York Times*, Mike Garafolo of the Newark *Star-Ledger*, and Paul Schwartz of the *Post*—all sat down with Coughlin, one-on-one, listening, listing complaints, trying to find common ground.

Stories of Coughlin as the model grandfather were peddled—the man known as the "Soup Nazi" was really "Pop-Pop," who would sit on the floor and play with toy trains for hours.

And, at the outset of the 2007 season, that new image was put to the test. The Giants lost the first two games. Eli Manning was maddeningly inconsistent right through November—when it appeared all was lost. On the final Sunday of that month, he threw a bucket full of interceptions in an embarrassing loss to the Minnesota Vikings, piloted by quarterback Tavaris Jackson, right in front of the grumbling Big Blue faithful at Giants Stadium, which emptied in the fourth quarter. But through it all, Coughlin remained remarkably calm. He didn't blow a gasket on the sideline. He didn't storm out on the press.

So, as the volatile 2007 season came to a merciful close, here was Coughlin and his team, which had secured the fifth seed in the NFC playoff picture by grinding out a victory in the snow in Buffalo. And, in the final game of the season, against ironically the undefeated New England Patriots at Giants Stadium, Coughlin had to make a choice—take the night off, or do what he's always done. Should Coughlin rest some of his weary veteran starters, he would make it easier for the Patriots to be the first team to finish 16–0. He would get no complaint from the fans or his critics who could fully justify his reasoning: another starter gets hurt, and the quest for the Super Bowl might be undone. What's more, this is what the new Coughlin could rationalize doing. In the end, isn't this what a player's coach is supposed to do—take care of his players?

But then he could hear his father. Back in 1961, young Tom had a big game for Waterloo Central High School in upstate New York, and on his way home he had heard nothing but praise from the townsfolk and friends. But when he got home, Lou was there with a much different view: "If that's the hardest you're going to play," his father said to him, "then you ought to find something else to do."

So, four days before the Saturday night showdown with the Patriots, Coughlin gathered his team and told them what the New York Giants were going to do. The announcement was really no surprise. Many of the veterans, even the oft-injured running back Brandon Jacobs, and the elder statesman, defensive end Michael Strahan, who could use the night off, had been lobbying the assistant coaches from the moment the Giants clinched a playoff spot the previous Sunday afternoon. They wanted to play. The last thing the veterans wanted to do was watch Tom Brady and Randy Moss and Tedy Bruschi and Bill Belichick iridescently and smugly hug it out after salting away the undefeated season, while the Giants' veterans tried to stay warm in street clothes on the bench. That was not happening.

"We will treat this like another game," is all Coughlin said. And there was not a single cheer or high-five in the room. And that's when Coughlin realized what had happened—by filing down the edges of his tyrannical approach, he had succeeded in bringing a certain undeniable autonomy and toughness to his players. They had taken ownership for what the coach had expected of them. Tom Coughlin, father figure.

Lou Coughlin would have been proud.

———

In the game of American football, the notion of coach as father figure was not created by accident.

From the earliest days of transition to the new game, Walter Camp lectured and wrote that soccer and rugby were haphazard—and, he thought, unfulfilling for the competitors and the spectators.

A modern rewriting of the history of American football says that the game naturally evolved out of rugby and soccer. Nothing could be further from the truth. In America, those games were rejected. Camp, for one, saw early on that their potential was limited in developing athletic skill and generating a large, dedicated fan base.

"His nickname, interestingly enough, was 'the Father of Football,'" said Robert Carroll, the lead historian at the Pro Football Researchers Association, a society of amateur football historians living in western Pennsylvania, the cradle of the pro game. "It was all about giving the coach a much more central role. It's really why it's football instead of soccer and rugby. In this country, we wanted more control, more strategy."

Camp's protégé, Amos Alonzo Stagg, took the lead in developing on-field strategy. At the University of Chicago, he invented line shifts (1897), the lateral pass (1898), the man in motion (1899), the unbalanced offensive line (1900), and the backfield shift (1904). But Stagg went further. He was the first to really implement Camp's push for more organization and innovation to help augment the changes on the field. Stagg was the first to put lights on the practice field to hold drills at night (1901), to award letters to varsity players (1906), and then numbering players (1913). (In baseball, by the way, Stagg invented the indoor batting cage—hey, it's cold in Chicago well into April—and pioneered the head-first slide.)

And he never stopped tinkering with football formations. In 1927, he came up with something called the 6-2-1-2 defense, putting six defenders on the line of scrimmage to put as much pressure as possible on the offense, especially the quarterback.

Indeed, the American game of football being played in the Midwest was always one step ahead of the Ivy Leagues and schools back East—mostly due to Stagg's innovations. It's widely assumed that Notre Dame wasn't much of a football school until Knute Rockne arrived in 1918. Not so. The Fighting Irish annihilated Army 35–13 in 1913 because of their innovative use of the passing game.

All these changes were brought on by better coaching—better organization, practices, and tactics. But there was one severe limitation. Coaching from the sideline during the game was prohibited. The narrative on the field was controlled by the players, particularly the quarterback. This was the essence of the American game.

Take, for example, Rockne—the first great father figure of American sports. Rockne, who compiled a 105–12–5 record at Notre Dame from 1918 to 1930, was a first-rate orator, a great motivator—using praise, disapproval, sarcasm, and anger to push, push, and push his players until he got the results he wanted. Sounds like Lombardi and Parcells, doesn't it? But Lombardi and Parcells could coach from the sideline. Rockne could not. Rockne had to rely on what he said during practice and, of course, in the locker room, to get his players to execute what he had designed.

"Rock was a great believer in the power of words," sportswriter Jack Newcombe wrote in *Sport* magazine in 1953. "He knew that the right word at the right time might do more for a lagging lineman than hours of sweat on the tackling dummy or the blocking machine.... He could be soothingly gentle or brutally scornful. He practiced such ego-smashing stunts as playing the Four Horsemen in a practice scrimmage behind a third-string line, and then snapping the star back fielders, 'Show 'em your clippings, boys.'"

But the Four Horsemen received no such coaching during the game. At the time, football rules—in college and in the fledgling pro league—would not let a coach shout instructions from the sideline. Substitutions of players were only after injury. A coach could not send in a play, could not even communicate with the players on the field during the game. In 1905, attempts at circumventing this rule were so rampant that the Intercollegiate Football Association changed it from a five-yard to a 10-yard penalty. In 1914, in fact, the association changed the rules so that everyone on the sideline must be seated on the team bench. First five men, then just three were allowed to walk up and down the sideline—all to put a stop to clandestine coaching during the game.

To be sure, coaches still tried to bend the rules. As substitution rules became more liberal, coaches would try to relay plays or instructions to the field. But rules in both college and professional football were specifically designed to prevent abuses: "Incoming substitutes are prevented from communication with their team on the field until after the first play," the college rule book stated.

"So, you had referees sometimes in the huddle, sometimes outside close by, listening to what was being said, looking for eye movements, blinking, anything to signal the next play," said historian Carroll. Penalties were assessed. But it was a judgment call, and that often led to major disputes, complaints, and protests. Nevertheless, the game's founders refused to bend. They were concerned about undue interference with the players on the field.

That's why Rockne's halftime speeches and antics were so important—and became so legendary. Rockne, the son of a carriage maker from Norway, the quintessential immigrant's son who fell in love with the new American game, gave many celebrated performances in the Notre Dame locker room—none more famous than the one he delivered at Yankee Stadium at halftime of a game against Army.

We're talking here about "Win one for the Gipper." George Gipp was a terrific running back who was a great improviser on the field. Rockne fell in love with his toughness, smarts, and versatility. But after the 1920 season, Gipp died after contracting pneumonia—complications after a tonsillectomy. Eight years later, in the midst of his worst season at Notre Dame, Rockne was in the halftime locker room with his team, which was getting embarrassed by a far superior Army squad in front of a sellout crowd in The House That Ruth Built.

That's when he trotted out the George Gipp story. He told the team that on his death bed, Gipp made two requests: to become a Catholic and that someday, when Notre Dame was facing impossible odds, he wished that Rockne would ask the team to win the game for him. "This," Rockne told them, "is that game." New York Mayor Jimmy Walker, who was in a corner of the locker room watching the whole scene, was overcome with emotion. Police officers guarding the door were crying. Notre Dame won the game 12–6.

That scene was immortalized in the Pat O'Brien movie version of Rockne's life. It created on the screen the first indelible image of the football coach not only as motivator, but, more important, as confessor—indeed, a priest, hearing a dying man's words and relaying them in such a way that it moved men to prevail against impossible odds. In short, the coach as mythic father figure.

As powerful as that was, the football coach as father figure was mostly confined to what the players saw and heard on the practice field and in the locker room. On Saturday and Sunday afternoons in both the college and pro games, spectators still very much focused on the players—not the coaches. For the most part, the coaches were still sitting on the bench, only occasionally on the sideline, still hamstrung by the prohibition against coaching during the game.

The emergence of the football coach as a powerful, daily symbol of the American patriarch really did not occur until after World War II.

And it all began with a simple rule change in 1944—in pro football.

———

World War II almost put an end to the NFL. Attendance dropped. The draft eviscerated team rosters. In 1943, the Cleveland Rams, one of the league's weaker teams, shut down operations. The Philadelphia Eagles merged with the Pittsburgh Steelers, becoming the Steagles. The Brooklyn Dodgers team would fold. The NFL considered shutting down.

In 1944, with a shortage of experienced manpower, the league had to do something to keep the product on the field at a high level. Detroit Lions owner Fred Mandel made a suggestion to Bears owner George Halas, who was still the NFL's numero uno: allow coaching during the game from the sideline.

"It was right in the middle of the war and players had much less experience," said football historian Robert Carroll. "You had a hard time fielding a full squad. So, it was natural to just let coaches be more involved in the game."

Within two years, one man would single-handedly change the image of the football coach in America. Wearing the trench coat and fedora of a businessman on the sideline, he cut the figure of a military officer, fully in charge of his men and his mission. He was the perfect portrait of the successful man in postwar America. His name was Paul Brown, and he built what is arguably pro football's greatest dynasty that practically nobody remembers: the Cleveland Browns from 1946 to 1955.

Let's remember what was happening during this time period. Thousands and thousands of GIs had returned home from the war, many of them having their one and only experience with military structure and institutions, coming back to a country changed radically by the government programs of the Roosevelt presidency. There was an expectation that the government would provide a safety net—the GI Bill helped do that.

The nation was fully engaged in the Cold War with the Soviet Union. Fear of communism ushered the Republican Party into the White House. In 1952, America elected the Supreme Commander of the Allied Forces in Europe, General Dwight D. Eisenhower, as president a full seven years after the war was over. It was the first time American voters had sent a decorated military hero directly to the White House since the Civil War.

Roosevelt proclaimed, "We have nothing to fear but fear itself" in 1941—a decade later, the country was looking for political shelter from fear, both real and imagined. Father figures fit the bill. It was a world of Republicanism—with a capital R.

It is against that backdrop that the situational comedy *Father Knows Best* debuted in 1949—first on radio. It's interesting that the radio program, also starring Robert Young as insurance salesman

Father Knows Best, *starring Robert Young, became one of the most-watched television programs of the 1950s.*

Jim Anderson from Springfield, Ohio, contained a question mark at the end of the title: *Father Knows Best?* But once it moved to CBS Television, all doubt disappeared—the question mark was removed. And *Father Knows Best* became one of the most-watched programs of the 1950s, and a symbol for American television of that era.

"At school in those days we lived in fear, our fear of teachers and grades were dwarfed by the fear of World War III or the H-bomb or the missiles that we daily expected Cold War hostilities would send from the dreaded Communists," essayist Susan Cheever wrote about *Father Knows Best.* "The Andersons represented the best of the American family, living in a world where difficulties were always learning experiences. They were what we wanted to be...."

These days, television is replete with dysfunctional father figures. The bad patriarch is everywhere, from Tony Soprano to Homer Simpson. On the show *Father Knows Best*, here was the ebullient Robert Young, with his open face of reassurance, anchoring a family—indeed, a nation—looking for direction, dovetailing almost seamlessly with the political slogan that got Eisenhower elected to two consecutive terms: "We Like Ike." While Robert Young's Jim Anderson coddled his daughter and would let his wife, played by Jane Wyatt, rule the roost, his fatherly advice for his oldest son, Bud, never wavered from the traditional role of the official Republican dad.

This all provided the ideal cultural environment for the patriarchal figure to really come to life in the game of football. And Paul Brown led the way.

Brown, a quarterback at the University of Miami in Ohio, was a very successful coach at Ohio State University. When the Cleveland Rams moved to Los Angeles, a new pro football league was started with the franchise in Cleveland as lynchpin. The industrial soul of eastern Ohio would support a pro football team—if it were any good. The new owners named Paul Brown to run the franchise. Good choice.

Brown immediately modernized the game and opened it up, literally and figuratively. He brought the first African American players in 13 years—Bill Willis and Marion Motley—back to pro football. The teams he assembled—117 players from 1946 to 1955—were from all walks of American life, every possible ethnic background: Hungarian, Irish, Italian, Polish, Armenian, Lithuanian, and Czech.

All this diversity needed a strong father figure. But Brown stressed teamwork and preparation in a way that wasn't necessarily dictatorial. Many of his players were World War II combat veterans. They didn't need another drill sergeant barking orders. They probably wouldn't have responded. Brown was a teacher, a clinician. He stressed hard work and discipline, yes, but he wanted his players to be prepared in a way that stressed the smallest details.

Brown stressed the gathering of every possible bit of intelligence about the opposition. Scouting became a science. (Steve Belichick, a Croatian from Youngstown, Ohio, who would coach at the Naval Academy for more than 30 years, wrote only one book, called *Football Scouting Methods*. One of the jacket quotes came from Paul Brown: "Scouting is essential football coaching.") Along with the emphasis on scouting was the complete devotion to film study.

In every word he delivered to his new team, Brown sounded like a father figure. He expected them to keep their notebooks neat. He wanted their personal lives to be clean. "Don't set up any love nests in Cleveland," he warned his players. "If you sneak out after bed checks, you'll be fined, and you'll read about it in the paper, and I'll be the first to tell your wife."

He wanted his players to wear a sport shirt to dinner, which was, he told them, "no place for pigs.... Class always shows."

"The Browns were in Philadelphia and the night before the game, all the Eagles were in the hotel bar drinking and Brown led his team right past them—they were all going to a movie together,"

Paul Brown served as head coach and father figure for the Cleveland Browns from 1946 to 1962.

said Jack Whitaker, who did the play-by-play for Eagles games on CBS.

Following the NFL's lead, the new league allowed sideline coaching, and Brown was a pioneer. So, it was on game day that Brown started to make real innovations. He mastered the T-formation offense and recruited quarterback Otto Graham to run it. From the sideline, Brown called the plays. "Sometimes, Otto would call an audible, but never often," said historian Carroll. "That's why he got the nickname 'Automatic Otto.'"

Brown used a so-called two-guard system, shuttling offensive linemen in and out of the game with his plays. (One of those guards was a guy named Chuck Noll.) This allowed the Browns to be more daring—often throwing the football when for years tradition told coaches and quarterbacks to quick-kick it. Third-and-long was a passing down for Graham. And with Motley's speed and size, the Browns wore down the opposition, giving Graham more and more opportunities to unload the ball deep.

Of all the changes Brown introduced, shuttling in players to call plays was the most revolutionary from a game day standpoint. For the first time, everybody in the stadium—the players, the opposition, both coaching staffs, the spectators, and, most of all, the members of the press—were watching a coach *coach*. From the opening whistle to the final gun, Brown was in total control. Many other coaches, from Stagg to Blaik, had been in control before, but here was an opportunity for everybody to see it. And it created a very powerful image. The trench coat. The fedora. There was no mistaking who knew best here. It was Paul Brown.

Brown was so consumed with controlling the action from the sideline that his shuttle system would often become cumbersome and delay the action on the field. So, in 1955, Brown experimented with a crude coach-to-quarterback radio communication system—40 years before the NFL approved its use. Unfortunately for Brown, the system was just not ready for prime time. In fact, the Giants caught wind of Brown's secret communication system and they intercepted the signals. The following year, league commissioner Bert Bell thought the whole idea violated the traditions of the game and the tenets of fair play. He banned it.

But that didn't stop the Browns' juggernaut. Otto Graham, old No. 14, earned more All-Pro honors and MVP awards and led his team to more championships than any quarterback in pro football history. Lou Groza, one of the greatest place-kickers ever, was perhaps the best offensive tackle of his generation, using his speed, size, and precision to clear a path for Motley. The sight of the powerful Motley charging around the end and down the sideline made defensive players cringe. On defense, Bill Willis used his speed, positioning, and leverage techniques devised by Brown's coaching staff—which at the time was the largest in pro football—to terrorize running backs. All four of them were enshrined in the Pro Football Hall of Fame in Canton, Ohio.

The Cleveland Browns thoroughly dominated the All-America Football Conference, outclassed the competition in every way—from how they played to how they conducted themselves on and off the football field. From 1946 to 1949, the Browns went an astonishing 47–4–3, winning four straight AAFC titles. Imagine that for a moment—in four years of football, the Browns lost only four games. In 1948, they went 14–0—24 years before the Miami Dolphins went undefeated.

In 1949, the AAFC folded. Three teams were absorbed by the NFL: the San Francisco 49ers, the Baltimore Colts, and the Browns. The NFL also took several star players from AAFC teams, including a defensive back from the New York Yankees by the name of Tom Landry.

The NFL fathers thought they were getting a new set of patsies. Wrong. The Browns were for real. The Giants, the Bears and the Eagles, who won the NFL championships of 1948 and 1949, were not ready for what came next. In 1950, their first year in the league, the Browns won the NFL title. That's five straight titles in two different leagues. From 1946 to 1955, Paul Brown's team went 105–17–4. The Browns are one of only four franchises in professional sports history to win five consecutive league titles, along with the Yankees (1949–1953), Boston Celtics (1959–1966), and Montreal Canadiens (1956–1960).

In 1954 and 1955, the Browns repeated as NFL champs. In fact, Cleveland reached the NFL title game in each of their first six seasons. In other words, Brown waltzed into an established league and just ate it alive.

But Cleveland's dynasty came to an abrupt end in 1956—the year Paul Brown met his equal: Tom Landry, who invented the 4-3 defense for the New York Giants.

That year, at Landry's behest, the Giants drafted a linebacker named Sam Huff. Landry made the rookie the anchor of his new defense, putting him at middle linebacker. And with Vince Lombardi running the Giants offense, and Landry pulling the strings on defense, the Giants won their first NFL title in 30 years.

In 1958, after Eisenhower was elected to a second term, America was turning on their TV sets every Monday night at 8:30 PM to watch Robert Young star in *Father Knows Best* on CBS. It was the perfect confluence of politics, culture, and sports. CBS Television was headquartered in Manhattan, on Sixth Avenue and 52nd Street. And the Giants played in New York, at Yankee Stadium in the Bronx. And there was a new face prowling the sideline, his eyes partially hidden by the brim of his fedora—Tom Landry.

He was stoic and clean-cut—just like Ike. He was an innovative coach—just like Brown. And, every week, he was there for all of America to watch in action—just like Robert Young.

"You watched Landry, you could not help but think of Brown—they were one and the same," said Whitaker, who broadcast NFL games on CBS for more than 20 years. "Landry was the coach in charge, and he looked the part on that sideline."

———

Thomas Wade Landry, the son of a mechanic and volunteer fireman from Mission, Texas, earned his wings at Lubbock Army Air Field and was sent to England, where he served in the 493rd Bomb Group, one of the most decorated squadrons in World War II. As a copilot in the 860th Bomb Squadron, Landry flew 30 missions, bombing

German garrisons, surviving a crash landing in Belgium after his B-17 ran out of fuel.

Returning from the war, he went back to playing football at the University of Texas. He was a fraternity brother. He got his degree in industrial engineering. And he spent many, many hours working for his church, The Lutheran Church-Missouri Synod of Texas. Not your typical football player.

In the pros, Landry shifted from fullback to defensive back first for the New York Yankees in the AAFC, then the New York Giants, making All-Pro in 1954. Head coach Jim Lee Howell recognized right away that Landry was meant to lead men, and he assigned him as a player/coach in 1955. The following year Landry was promoted to defensive coordinator, giving him a chance to use his 4-3 defense, which was primarily designed to stop Paul Brown's punishing but lightning-quick offense, which had just won the NFL championship in back-to-back seasons.

Landry admired Brown. Studied everything he did. Watched his every move on the sideline. Like Brown, Landry was placid and keen, but, without notice, he could turn tough and demanding. And, like Brown, he fancied himself an innovator. And what better way to show that you know best than beating the father at his own game? So, in the era when coaching from the sidelines was beginning to develop into its current state of performance art, and television was beginning to take notice, Tom Landry was the first defensive coach as a symbol for the times, and for where the game was headed.

"The game really changed then, and the focus was no longer just up and down the field, but sideline to sideline," said Whitaker. "You had to pay attention to what was going on on the sideline, or you would miss a lot of the action. This was a big change. And it helped TV tell the story through the coaches' eyes." The changes in the game wrought by coaching from the sideline forced the new storyteller—television—to widen its field of vision. It gave the narrative more depth. Indeed, it would not take long for the viewer to become an arm-chair coach. From the comfort of the living room, the fan could now proclaim a stake in the story—by identifying with the coach, what the coach did, what moves he made, how he controlled the pace of the game.

It helped, too, that this was all happening in New York, with Madison Avenue watching. But Landry also had a separate set of obstacles because he was in New York. His opposite number on the Giants sideline was Vince Lombardi, the offensive coordinator who had his own set of ambitions. Making matters worse, team owner Wellington Mara loved Lombardi—they shared that Fordham University Jesuit bond, a clannish connection that Mara leaned on when Lombardi considered leaving the Giants in 1955 (Mara talked him out of it).

So, Landry needed a bold stroke. And the 4-3 defense was it. The idea was to drop off the ends of the six-man defensive line to stop the sweep that Brown had perfected with Motley. "What everybody was doing was forcing the play back inside, but Tom came up with the idea of defending the end run inside-out, stopping opponents up the middle with the idea that pursuit would take care of the outside," said Wellington Mara. "The four defensive linemen were charged with the responsibility of keeping the five offensive linemen from getting a clear shot at the middle linebacker."

Landry wanted to repeat on defense what Brown had done on offense. The man with the degree in industrial engineering was going to add scientific method to the brutish side of the ball.

"The offense has its plays diagrammed for it and knows ahead of time what to do," Landry said much later in life. "The defense must constantly anticipate and react. On defense, you have to accept the fact that you're going to give the other guy the first shot. The initial advantage is his. I just always have had an analytical mind and this was most intriguing for me."

Landry said it was becoming obvious watching Brown use Motley that "the thing to do was to keep the ends dropped off, covering the flare areas, making them linebackers. But what I needed was a guy in the middle who was pretty quick, pretty active, and could key."

That guy was Sam Huff. He was mobile and he was tough. "It's uncanny the way Huff follows the ball," said Lombardi. "He's all over the field all at once." On the field, Huff became Landry's quarterback. "Sam was excellent at following instructions," said Landry. "He was very disciplined and he would listen... Most defensive players get hit and fight through the block. We hold. We do not fight through the block. We control an area. That's based on my engineering background, coordinating people."

By design, Landry was staking his claim as the next Paul Brown—the next dominant patriarchal figure in professional football. By comparison, Lombardi was mercurial and profane—the way he looked and acted said Brooklyn. Landry was even-tempered and never raised his voice. Straight as they come.

"Some of us would go off for a beer but Tom would just disappear, go off with his family," said Hall of Fame defensive back Emlen Tunnell. "I had a lot of respect for him." Many years later, Landry's image never wavered. "Every road trip, every away game, you got on the team bus and there was Tom and his wife, Alicia, sitting in seats 1A and 1B on the plane, dressed impeccably," said Brian Baldinger, who played under Landry for six years in Dallas in the 1980s. "And it sent a powerful message of how we were expected to act as players and as men. You wore a coat and tie on the road, you looked like Tom Landry. You acted like Tom Landry."

Landry could've stepped right off the sideline and onto the set of fictional Springfield, Ohio, with "Bud," and "Kitten" and "Princess," and shouted "Honey, I'm home!" and not missed a beat.

In 1956, the first year the Giants played at Yankee Stadium, Landry turned his new defense piloted by his rookie middle linebacker into a dominant force. Two new defensive linemen—Andy Robustelli, brought over from the Rams, and Dick Modzelewski, acquired from the Steelers—gave Huff all the protection he needed. That year, the Giants gave up just 3.5 yards per rush, tied for tops in the league. And New York finished 8–3 to win the Eastern Conference.

And it was all captured by America's Tiffany Network, the Columbia Broadcasting System (CBS). The network signed a new deal to broadcast all NFL games nationwide. America could watch Robert Young during the week, and Paul Brown and Tom Landry and Vince Lombardi on Sunday afternoons.

It was Landry's defense that stole the show. In the NFL Championship Game of 1956—broadcast live across the nation— the powerful Monsters of the Midway, which led the league with a 9–2–1 record and scored a league-high 363 points, were held to just one touchdown. Chicago's offense was so battered that George Halas abandoned the T-formation when the Bears returned to the field after halftime. With a sellout crowd jammed into the Big Ballpark in the Bronx, the Giants won 47–7. Father Tom had beaten Papa Bear.

In one season as defensive coordinator, playing with a rookie middle linebacker in a completely new defensive system, Tom Landry enjoyed a meteoric rise to national prominence that would eventually land him the top job with the new franchise in Dallas four years later.

In 1960, Tom Landry left the New York Giants.

In 1960, Robert Young left the show *Father Knows Best*.

With Landry, CBS had a new leading man for a whole new American narrative, a new show on a new team in a new state in America's heartland. In his home state, wearing a fedora and a suit and tie and a nicely trimmed overcoat if needed, Landry piloted the Dallas Cowboys just like he pictured it growing up in Mission, Texas. He took the Cowboys to five Super Bowl games, winning Super Bowl VI in 1971 and Super Bowl XII in 1977, winning an astonishing 270 games. He had 20 consecutive winning seasons, and was inducted into the Pro Football Hall of Fame in 1990.

Lombardi had much more success in a shorter period, but he died in 1970. Landry coached nearly 20 more years, a symbol of steady sideline stewardship through the turbulent 1970s and the wide-open 1980s. Landry was a fixture in America's homes every Sunday afternoon, fulfilling that image of the football patriarch. He was the common thread that ran through all the economic and political turmoil of a turbulent time that spanned nearly three decades.

And the Cowboys were "America's Team" in America's Game— just as *Father Knows Best* was America's television program. The team and show—with Landry and Young as the patriarchs— symbolized what America thought about itself, what it thought it wanted to be.

———

Of course, it's never that easy. Nor should it be. It's easier for us to create myths, perpetuate illusions. For some reason, it has always been important for America to share a pop culture that was created for commercial purposes. In the 1950s, pro football was being recreated for commercial purposes right in America's living rooms.

Not everybody went along. Miles Davis described the '50s this way: "People were reacting to the packaging of American life. They wanted something elegant, but with a bite to it."

Jim Brown provided the bite.

And then Johnny Unitas broke off the whole meal.

After Landry's defense embarrassed the Bears in the 1956 NFL Championship Game on national television, Paul Brown, watching at home in Cleveland, immediately formulated Plan B. And Plan B was Jim Brown. The plan was to draft Brown out of Syracuse and jackhammer the 4-3 defense, especially Huff. It worked.

In the 14 regular season games where Huff went up against Jim Brown, the Cleveland running back averaged a whopping five yards per carry. In 1957, with a record of 9–2–1, the Browns finished ahead of the Giants in the Eastern Conference. The Detroit Lions won the NFL Championship Game that season, beating Cleveland 59–14.

Landry's defense in New York would return to the NFL Championship Game, but in both 1958 and 1959, his 4-3 defense was solved by Johnny Unitas. With Baltimore Colts head coach Weeb Ewbank growling petulantly on the sideline, Unitas—in one dramatic moment on national television in what is called The Greatest Game Ever Played—threw off the yoke of Paul Brown and Tom Landry, of the coach on the sideline always in total control on the field.

By calling his own plays as he drove down the field twice to beat the Giants in the dusk of Yankee Stadium and prevail in overtime, Unitas was not only putting the game of pro football on the national map in a historic stroke of genius, he was also challenging an idea of how football in the decade of the 1950s had come to explain America.

At the founding of the American game of football, Camp and Stagg had set a course on parallel tracks: the coach and the quarterback would be the central players in this new sporting narrative. Coaching would modernize the European game, add intrigue, innovation, and tactics. The quarterback would be the protagonist, the gunslinger who would make the spectators feel like it was their story, too.

Post World War II, the *Father Knows Best* era of American culture, the coach emerged as a dominant force. In the 1960s, the new generation—following Johnny U's lead—would struggle to take it back.

———

Tom Coughlin made the right call. Playing to win was the right move. While the standings said the New York Giants had nothing on the line, they proved to their coach they had everything to gain.

Coughlin's young quarterback, Eli Manning, played his best game of the season, throwing four touchdown passes, navigating through Tedy Bruschi and Rodney Harrison and Mike Vrabel and the rest of Bill Belichick's veteran defense to give the Giants a 12-point lead in the third quarter.

Unfortunately for New York, Tom Brady was the other quarterback. And he was not about to let this story, this historic narrative of an unbeaten season, end like this.

"Brady told us in the huddle at the beginning of the fourth quarter that we would come back," said Patriots offensive tackle Matt Light. "I don't remember the exact words. But I do remember the look on his face. He was pissed."

With patience and precision, Brady led the Patriots on an eight-play touchdown drive, at one point hitting on five straight passes from the shotgun, cutting the lead to three points at the end of the third quarter.

Getting the ball back in the fourth quarter, Brady saw the Giants' best cover cornerback, Sam Madison, leave the field, doubled over in agony from what would later be described as a stomach pull. Madison had been checking Randy Moss, and doing a pretty good job of it. Split wide right with Madison now on the bench, Moss streaked down the sideline, right in front of Coughlin and the rest of the Giants coaching staff. From the shotgun, Brady collected the ball and let it fly. Sixty-five yards later—touchdown. It was a record-setter: Brady's 50th touchdown pass of the year, setting a single-season record. It was Moss's 23rd touchdown reception of the year, also a single-season record. And it gave the Patriots a lead they never relinquished. Final score: 38–35.

But Coughlin's players found out something. They found out they could hang with the big bad Patriots. They found out they could respond to the pressure of playing for something more than what was obvious—what it said in the standings, what was being said in the media, what was said in the past.

They found out that Tom Coughlin knew best.

———

Postscript: Back to Paul Brown for a minute. Brown's aloof personality never won him any congeniality awards—just like a man who would study his methods many years later, Bill Belichick.

Brown suffered only one losing season in Cleveland. Nevertheless, new team owner Art Modell fired him in 1962, saying the game had passed Brown by. Years later, Brown would return to the NFL, taking the Cincinnati Bengals to two Super Bowls, losing both.

8

*"Now that you know who you are,
What do you want to be?"*

—Lennon & McCartney

How Football Explains
the '60s

The sun had long settled along the western Wisconsin plain, leaving Green Bay with no protection from the dark cold January night. The streets, including Vince Lombardi Avenue and Mike Holmgren Way, were slowly abandoned like a neighborhood that had been warned hours ago about the arrival of an impending storm. But the only thing brewing was a football game, a dramatic climax to the long, sometimes tortuous narrative of the 2007 NFL season.

Outside Lambeau Field, the national cathedral of American football, a bank sign ominously flashed the temperature: minus-1 degree. On the radio, they barked the wind chill, that measure of the Canadian Clipper when it streaks down through Lake Michigan, rips through the Lower Fox River, which cuts Green Bay in half, and collides with the cold air of northern Wisconsin. On this night, the people of Green Bay were happy to report the wind chill was minus-23 degrees.

Many of them had waited their whole lives to be part of something like this. They had all grown up hearing, over and over, about December 31, 1967, when the kickoff temperature was 13 below zero, and the wind chill minus-46, and the legends of Vince Lombardi and Bart Starr and Jerry Kramer were made after a quarterback sneak on a sheet of ice on "The Frozen Tundra" of Lambeau beat the Dallas Cowboys 21–17, sending the Packers to the Super Bowl in a game known simply as The Ice Bowl.

So, on the 40th anniversary of that championship season, more than 72,740 Packer fans shuffled into Lambeau Field, dressed in the layers of hunters and truck drivers and ice fishermen, with the anticipation of watching a little history that they could finally claim as their own.

January 20, 2008. The Green Bay Packers facing the New York Giants for the NFC championship.

Ice Bowl II.

Football is man against man and man against himself. But when you add a blast of inhumane artic cold to the equation, football becomes man against man, against himself, and against the forces of nature. This is what Walter Camp and the founding fathers of football had in mind when they forged this game—created a story line like that of the American pioneers navigating through the dangerous wilderness or across a treacherous plain.

And that's the story line that Fox Television was happy to promote. Any TV producer will tell you bad-weather games mean good ratings. The players are more passionate, the action more intense, and the audience can't look away. So there was Joe Buck, the play-by-play announcer from Fox who has no peer, telling his national audience that all the pieces were in place for one more great football drama—far from Hollywood's myth-making machinery, far from New York's myth-busting media. Here, in Green Bay, a cradle of the game, no script was necessary. Never was.

Of course, no one—not Buck, not the proud population of tiny Green Bay, not the tens of millions of Americans watching at home—could have scripted what would happen next: a surprise twist of an ending that would validate Tom Coughlin's coaching career, give Eli Manning a chance to live in the neighborhood of Joe Namath's legend, and unceremoniously force the end of the line for Brett Favre, whose lofty status in Green Bay approaches Vincehood itself.

The final scenes, now frozen for all time:

Lawrence Tynes, the Giants' frail-boned, Scottish-born place-kicker, driving his right leg into the football, pulling a 43-yard field goal wide left with 6:53 left in the fourth quarter, game tied 20–20, and Coughlin slapping the laminated play card into his hands, screaming at Tynes as he returned to his hooded parka on the sidelines, hoping for a second chance.

Six minutes and 49 seconds later: with just four seconds showing on the clock, Tynes swings his right leg into the frozen ball again, this time with way too much adrenaline, and the ball flutters harmlessly far left of the uprights, sending the story into the territory claimed previously only by Johnny Unitas in 1958— sudden-death overtime. And how fitting that is: Unitas of Baltimore, where the Giants general manager who picked Eli Manning—Ernie Accorsi—got his football career started.

And Manning, with his offensive coordinator Kevin Gilbride calling the plays, kept bringing the Giants back, giving Tynes more chances. Favre, who was supposed to ride this game into the fitting final act of a glorious career, appeared instead to be in a state of suspended animation. Here's how the Packers offense went in its final three drives with Favre in the pilot's seat: three plays and a punt; three plays and a penalty, then punt; one play, and then one of the worst passes in postseason history.

In overtime, the Packers won the toss, and Green Bay got the ball on their own 26-yard line. Running back Ryan Grant was stoned for just a two-yard gain—after halftime Grant had been held to just 17 yards on the ground.

So, Packers head coach Mike McCarthy—runner-up for NFL Coach of the Year honors—called on Favre to throw an out route to Donald Driver, even though Favre had completed just two of his last six pass attempts for 12 yards in the last 16 minutes and 26 seconds, a lifetime of championship football. Favre looked right at the receiver and let go of the football, but it was badly underthrown. Corey Webster broke in front of Driver and snatched the ball.

Four plays later, Tynes did not wait for Coughlin to send him on the field. He just ran right in front of the stunned head coach, whose face was a greasy red—covered in Vaseline to protect against frostbite, something his mother taught him growing up in upstate New York. Tynes, like he was going out for groceries, just casually walked up to the ball, placed down by punter Jeff Feagles, and kicked the game-winning 47-yard field goal, the first time that an opposing kicker had connected on a game-winner in overtime in Lambeau playoff history.

Manning rushed the field, bewildered. Michael Strahan ran after Manning and embraced him. "We're going to the Super Bowl," Strahan said. "I wanted this so bad." Strahan, denied once before, had talked all week to his friends, family, and teammates about going out a Super Bowl champion. Manning whispered in his ear: "We're going to getcha one. We're gonna getcha one."

"I love you, man," Strahan replied.

Favre, barely able to speak or move, caught up with Manning at about the 30-yard line. He congratulated Manning in a way that suggested to the young quarterback that Farve had nothing left, that another storied era in Green Bay Packers football had been defined and was now coming to an end.

Favre was now loser of three of his last five postseason games at Lambeau Field. Prior to those three losses, the Packers had gone through 81 years of football without losing a single playoff game on their home turf. More than eight decades without a loss—13–0.

That unbeaten streak is what created the legend of Lambeau, the mystique of playing in Titletown—so named in the grainy era of Curly Lambeau himself in the '30s, and then in the shadows of black-and-white TV in the late '50s, to the full "Lucy in the Sky with Diamonds" color of the Age of Aquarius, when a skinny son of an army master sergeant came out of Alabama to be the unlikely leader of a football team that would help define a turbulent decade of American sports.

Bart Starr and the Silent Majority

The story of football in America in the '60s really begins with a man in a flattop haircut, a military man through and through, who was raising two boys in Montgomery, Alabama, in the early 1950s.

Ben Starr, a master sergeant in the army, had two sons, the older, Bryan Bartlett "Bart," and younger Hilton "Bubba." And he ran his house like a military base. It was "yes, sir," and "no, sir" and "right away, sir"—the B-side of *Father Knows Best.*

And like any family you can name, the father rode the older son the hardest, constantly reminding him of how to act and what to do, and frequently reminding him that he was not doing enough to measure up. Tragically, Bart's younger brother died at the age of 13. Near their home, Bubba had been playing in an old ballfield and stepped on a dog bone, dying of tetanus three days later. This left Bart Starr to live up to all his father's demands and expectations.

He did what all young boys hoped to do growing up in Alabama—he went to play football for the Crimson Tide. But this was before Paul "Bear" Bryant was brought home to coach Alabama, and Starr's final two years in Montgomery did not go well. He was hurt his junior season and, in his senior year, the Tide did not win a game, going 0–10. And on NFL draft day in 1956— the year the Giants finally dispatched the Browns and won the NFL championship, and Mickey Mantle won the Triple Crown, and the whole world of American sports seemed to travel through the city of New York—Starr had to wait until the 17th round to hear his name called. And it was not by the Bears or the Browns or the

Giants, but by the Packers, a team that played football as far away from Montgomery as Starr could possibly imagine.

And for three years, while Unitas planted his flag in pro football immortality, Starr languished in Green Bay, where under head coaches Lisle Blackbourn and Scooter McLean, the Packers failed to have a winning season, finishing 1–10–1 in 1958. It was so bad for Starr in 1958 that Blackbourn, then at Marquette University, called Starr on the telephone right around Christmas and asked him if wanted to join his staff to coach the running backs. Starr was not about to quit. Good thing he didn't. A few days later, Vince Lombardi and his wife, Marie, packed up their belongings and left New Jersey to become the first family of football in Green Bay, Wisconsin.

"When I joined the team, the opinion around here and in the league was that Starr would never make it," said Lombardi. "They said he couldn't throw well enough and wasn't tough enough, that he had no confidence in himself, and no one had any confidence in him."

Lombardi said that after looking at the film of Starr's first three seasons, he saw a quarterback who could make all the throws and could handle the offense. "What he needed was confidence," said Lombardi. "When I first met him he struck me as so polite and so self-effacing that I wondered if maybe he wasn't too nice a boy to be the authoritarian leader your quarterback must be." When Lombardi was head coach at St. Cecilia's, he often called the Englewood police department to see if they had any truants or problem kids they could recommend for the football team. It was something he learned at Army from Red Blaik, who recruited heavily around New York, Philadelphia, and Pittsburgh, looking for tough working-class kids who might have had a few arrests for minor infractions.

But there were two qualities Starr possessed that impressed Lombardi. First, he had a terrific memory, and wasn't afraid to study all hours to master every nuance of Lombardi's playbook.

Second, Starr, a Methodist who has never been heard uttering a curse word, could take everything that the old foul-mouthed Jesuit from Brooklyn could dish out. Whatever Lombardi had to offer, Ben Starr had already delivered in triplicate. Bart Starr was made for Vince Lombardi. Ben Starr had seen to that.

And Starr was the perfect quarterback for America at the time. The Beatles had yet to cross the Atlantic. Vietnam was out of sight, out of mind. It was crew cuts and the space race. It was, metaphorically speaking, the night before going to college immortalized by George Lucas in his movie, *American Graffiti*— innocence not yet lost, questions not yet being asked.

The image of Starr was that he asked none—that with Lombardi, too, it was all "yes, sir," and "no, sir." Lombardi knew what it would take to win an NFL championship. He saw it firsthand in New York in 1956: a brutal defense, a dynamic running game, and a quarterback who does not make mistakes. And this is what the nation saw when Lombardi turned the Packers around, turned them into the preeminent football champion of a generation: Bart Starr quietly going about his business, the caretaker of a Hall of Fame roster, the unassuming steward of the regal Paul Hornung, the rabble-rousing Max McGee, the defiant Jerry Kramer, and their demonstrative head coach.

In 1965, another quarterback from the University of Alabama, Joe Namath, was drafted in the first round by the New York Jets of the American Football League. With glamorous fanfare, in the shadow of Broadway, Namath was made the highest-paid athlete in American sports. That same year, Starr set an NFL record by throwing 294 passes in a row without an interception. And the Packers won their third NFL championship in five years.

But Starr was no caretaker. He called his own plays. Day in, day out for more than half a decade, Starr studied game film more than any other player on the championship rosters of the Green Bay Packers—Lombardi himself attested to that. What Lombardi

Bart Starr led the Packers to five NFL championships and defined the Silent Majority of football in the 1960s.

always said separated Starr from every other quarterback of his generation was his ability to read defenses, call a play, and execute it at the critical juncture of a game.

"You've got to go with the plays that have worked in critical situations," said Starr. "Most fans do not realize how critical going into the end zone for a touchdown is. If a team gets down to the goal, and does not come away with seven, they're in trouble."

It was this precise thinking that catapulted Starr to the very top of his profession on December 31, 1967. Calling the plays on a field that felt like an aircraft carrier flight deck covered with ice, Starr led the Packers down the field in the fourth quarter to the doorstep of the Dallas Cowboys goal line with 16 seconds left in the NFL Championship Game.

The Packers were down by three points and could have elected to try a field goal. But the Packers under Lombardi with Starr at the helm were not accustomed to going for the tie, and anyway the field was deemed too slippery to change that philosophy now.

So Lombardi told Starr to run "31 Wedge," where running back Chuck Mercein, who had already made a critical catch and run during the final drive, would dive between the center and guard and score the winning touchdown in the most famous football game of the decade.

Starr called the play in the huddle. Then, when he got to the line of scrimmage, he did not like what he saw. Too slippery. What if Mercein couldn't get his footing? What if Starr turned around with the ball and Mercein was sprawled, facedown on the icy field? The Packers would have been out of timeouts and probably not had enough time to run another play, and the Cowboys would win, and instead of it being called the Lombardi Trophy, Tom Landry's name would be carved on the side of the Super Bowl hardware.

So, Starr changed the play, without telling a soul. He kept the football and dove behind Jerry Kramer—a quarterback sneak, a play the Packers did not even have in their playbook. On the sideline, Lombardi raised his arms: touchdown—Packers 21, Cowboys 17.

Still, to this day, on the credit scale for the Lombardi Era in Green Bay, Starr rarely rises to the top, rarely gets his due. Still called the caretaker. Still thought of as the silent partner, but in everything that was invested in the Packers' dynasty, Starr was clearly a majority stockholder.

In all, the Packers won five NFL championships. Starr was 9–1 in the postseason, throwing just three interceptions in 213 postseason pass attempts, still an NFL record. His quarterback rating in the postseason is 104.8—20 points higher than Favre's. (Thirty-eight points higher, by the way, than Johnny Unitas in the postseason.)

But Starr, who would sit in his room on the road and study the Bible, went down in history as a bit player in what the Packers accomplished. He owned no bars in midtown Manhattan like Namath. Women did not chase him from city to city. He had no appeal on Madison Avenue. He came to represent that portion of America in the 1960s that was supposed to have quietly supported the war in Vietnam—what Richard Nixon would later claim was the "Silent Majority." Ben Starr taught his son that it was impolite to challenge authority.

In a *Time* magazine article in 1971, political analyst Champ Clark wrote: "In its essence, the football audience is Middle America in the raw. It is the Silent Majority at its noisiest, relieving its frustration in the visual excitement of the nation's most popular sport."

The man who first used that term was Richard Nixon, in a speech on November 3, 1969—the year Joe Namath won Super Bowl III.

Joe Namath… "and Nixon's coming"
Don Meredith was leaving the *Monday Night Football* booth, and Howard Cosell was looking for his replacement. Cosell and Meredith

were two halves of a vaudevillian act on national television, a classic mix of red-state and blue-state sensibilities decades before those two terms were to be used: a liberal New York lawyer who antagonized the nation, and a sweet-talking "lower-case cowboy," as Cosell called him, who could call Cosell out with a five-word putdown that had the country talking the next morning.

Cosell needed a new partner, a new foil. Bart Starr wanted the job. "Bart Starr came in to see me," Cosell said. "On any list of the world's greatest gentlemen, put him at the top. He explained to me what he could bring to the package in terms of football analysis." Cosell told Starr that he would take his candidacy to Roone Arledge, the creator of *Monday Night Football* at ABC-TV. "I explained the type of performer that Roone was seeking," the late Cosell said in 1974. "Bart was not considered."

Starr did not fit the right demographic. Despite his name, he did not have the right star appeal, especially as the '60s came to a close. *Monday Night Football* had already proven to be irreverent— on one broadcast Meredith had referred to Nixon as "Tricky Dick." Nobody took his subsequent apology seriously.

The Watergate investigation was in full swing, a constant drumbeat of unanswered questions about the Nixon White House filled the nightly news. The Vietnam War was coming to a messy conclusion. On Monday night, prime-time football needed somebody who crossed all demographic lines. There was only one guy for that job: Joe Namath.

Monday Night Football had helped pro football overtake baseball as America's most popular sport. And Namath—ABC chose the New York Jets against the Cleveland Browns for the broadcast debut of *Monday Night Football*—was the game's biggest star. He sold everything from shaving cream to pantyhose. Namath may have been in the middle of a 13-year career in which he threw more touchdown passes than interceptions only twice. His career completion percentage is 50.1 percent. Starr was far more efficient,

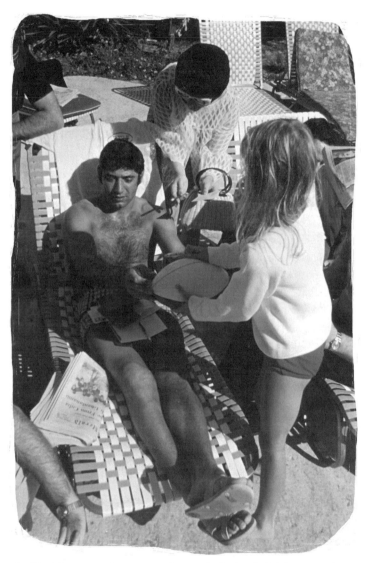

Joe Namath represented a new type of quarterback when he led the New York Jets to a legendary victory in Super Bowl III.

effective and productive and won five NFL titles. Namath may have won only one, but it was the biggest of them all, making the AFL-NFL merger legitimate and transforming pro football from a mere sport into an entertainment spectacle.

After he won Super Bowl III, Namath was as big as The Beatles. One night, in a Miami nightclub after the big game, Frank Sinatra came over to pay his respects to Namath. In Las Vegas, Elvis Presley stopped his act to lead the audience in a standing ovation when Namath walked into the room.

Out of the '60s, Namath symbolized the one pro football myth that might endure. Lombardi was dead. Starr was a symbol of the past, a Nixonian character at a time when the political guard was about to change. Namath, a renegade, had enough crossover appeal to bridge all demographic fiefdoms—in short, with Meredith leaving, Namath could build the biggest prime-time following.

"It is Namath who they want for the situation comedies and variety shows on television," Cosell said. "It is Namath who is advertised for his obvious sex appeal, and women do constitute a large part of our audience."

It's important to realize how much competitive pressure existed at that time in America's burgeoning television industry. It's a wonder that broadcasting professional sports flourished at all. At home, the American audience was bombarded with new images from all fronts—the struggles of the civil rights movement, unrest at college campuses, men going to the moon. Also, a constant carnival of entertainment programs competed for eyeballs every night. The fact that pro football found its niche on TV, cemented a loyal following, and grew its audience is a minor miracle. Baseball struggled. Basketball and hockey were not even considered much of a national broadcast product. College football foundered. What saved the NFL was the star power of prime-time broadcasts on Monday night. Roone Arledge and Howard Cosell built a bridge from the vanishing myths of the '60s to a decade that greeted the pervasiveness and power of professional sports, especially football, with more and more skepticism.

Arledge and Cosell wanted Namath so badly, they suggested that he keep playing on Sundays, then turnaround on Monday nights and hop in the booth. NFL commissioner Pete Rozelle did not object. But the Jets said no—Namath was the team's property. With his knees giving way, and his career spiraling downward, Namath was still in a Jets uniform because, well, there was no clean way to dispose of a national icon and your only marketable product. Namath still put fannies in the seats. And the Jets did not want to share that commodity.

Namath's representatives told Cosell to tell Arledge to tell the Jets "to go to hell," Cosell said.

So in 1974, Meredith was replaced by former Detroit Lions defensive lineman Alex Karras—not exactly a household name. Cosell, desperate to recreate some of the magic of the earlier days, went searching for star power to invite to the booth. His biggest get was John Lennon, who ironically once said, "Take the politics out of your art, and you're basically left with TV."

Live on national TV, Lennon got his first exposure to American football. But not without some politics thrown in. That night, Frank Gifford's guest was the former governor of California, Ronald Reagan. Before the game, the man who played the Gipper in the movies gave Lennon a crash course in the rules of football, and how and why it was so big in America. It was a spontaneous, but near-perfect blend of all of football's demographics—Lennon, the de facto leader of the counterculture movement; Reagan, the political heir to the Silent Majority; and the *Monday Night Football* broadcast using an old actor who once played a famous college football player telling Liverpool's most famous son why America loves its indigenous game.

Lennon loved it. He liked a good show. And that's what football was becoming.

But not to everybody.

Football Freaks

It really all started with Harry Edwards, who in 1968 created the Olympic Project for Human Rights. Edwards failed to bring a boycott of the Olympic Games in Mexico City, but his was the first organization to really use sports as a vessel of political organization on a national scale.

Edwards's nascent movement, which began in the San Francisco Bay Area, quickly spread, growing alongside the student movement, the black liberation movement, and the antiwar protests of the time. By 1967, "well over 100 athletic programs at major colleges and universities" had been rocked by some form of disturbance, according to a study done by Jack Scott at the Institute for the Study of Sport and Society in Oakland, California. By fall of 1969, the problem was so widespread that *Sports Illustrated* published a three-part series called "The Desperate Coach."

Pro football was right in the middle of it. In 1970, Dave Meggyesy, a former linebacker for the then–St. Louis Cardinals, wrote a scathing attack on the NFL called *Out of My League*. Meggyesy introduces his book by talking about the haunting images of blowing out an opponent's knee on a low block during a kick-off return on a rainy afternoon in St. Louis. "The conditions that made me feel a confused joy at breaking up another man's body gradually became just one of the many reasons why I decided to quit the game."

For the first time ever, the game was being de-mythologized by the very men who had created a powerful national passion for it. This was a new part of the literature of American football: rebellion. Not just wearing fur coats on the sideline or defying the commissioner of pro football by owning a bar with a bunch of gamblers—like Namath did. This was a push for social change through sports.

"By exposing the change potential of sport," said Edwards, "it opened the door for all these traditionally excluded groups to begin to pursue and push their interest."

In football, like in baseball, there was a labor movement. But while baseball players would soon win free agency following the Curt Flood decision, football players would have to wait two more decades to achieve a similar level of economic power and freedom. More than anyone, Meggyesy captured the mood. "After playing the sport most of my life, I've come to see that football is one of the most dehumanizing experiences a person can face," he said.

"You've got to remember what was happening at the time in the country," said professor Michael Oriard of Oregon State, who played center for the Kansas City Chiefs in the early 1970s. "We were dealing with the Vietnam War. A generation of young men viewed the military and pro football in the same way, as destructive and dehumanizing. Football was another extension for explaining what was happening in America."

It all came back to the win-at-all-costs mentality created around Lombardi. Players were seen as interchangeable parts, disposable elements of a team that had one goal: defeat was not an option. Pediatric sociologists started writing and lecturing about the harmful impact it was said to be having on America's youth.

In an essay called "The Destructive Pro Model," Dr. Thomas Tutko wrote, "there is a win-at-all-costs lunacy which sets the competitive tenor for many of the adults who run our childhood sports programs. We have already seen how this obsession with success can be rationalized at the professional level and [that] philosophy is now contaminating play at the Pop Warner level."

Tutko argued this "poison" circled back to Lombardi. Meggyesy blamed somebody else.

"To me, it is no accident that Richard Nixon, the most repressive president in American history, is a football freak, and that the sport is rapidly becoming our version of bread and circuses," he said.

In another time, perhaps, Meggyesy might have been a Nixon guy. He was born and raised in Cleveland. His parents were Hungarian, clearly card-carrying members of the Silent Majority.

He was an immigrant's son who gravitated toward the game to assimilate into American society. But at the time Meggyesy wrote his book, Nixon represented something entirely different and his association with football helped explain the generation gap.

Nixon called Washington Redskins head coach George Allen to congratulate the team—and suggest plays. He used football terms in his prosecution of the Vietnam War. When he ordered mines planted in Haiphong Harbor in North Vietnam in 1972, that illegal escalation of the war was called "Operation Linebacker."

And Nixon loved Lombardi—"the patron saint of American competition," as his biographer Maraniss so aptly called him. Lombardi's slogans were being adopted by business leaders and politicians across America. In the Washington office of CREEP, the Committee to Re-Elect the President, a Nixon operative hung a sign that read: "Winning in Politics Isn't Everything. It's the Only Thing."

After leaving Green Bay in 1968, Lombardi quickly returned to coaching by taking the titles of vice president and head coach of the Washington Redskins, arriving in the nation's capital the same year as Nixon—1969. On the surface, it appeared that Nixon and Lombardi were, indeed, one and the same. Both worried that the counterculture movement was unraveling core Middle American values. In 1968, the *Milwaukee Sentinel*, in an editorial, said out loud what a lot of people had been thinking: that Lombardi should run for public office. "He is articulate in matters of national concern," the newspaper said.

Indeed, in 1968, Nixon dispatched the man who would later become his attorney general, John Mitchell, to investigate the possibility of Lombardi being his running mate in 1968. But the Nixon campaign was disappointed. Mitchell found that Lombardi, like many urban Catholics from the Northeast, was a Democrat. His parents voted for Franklin Roosevelt. In 1960, he voted for John F. Kennedy, whose love for football was well documented (all of America had seen the black-and-white photos of the Kennedy clan playing touch football at the family compound on Cape Cod). Shortly after taking office, Kennedy met Lombardi at a football banquet in New York. They hit it off and kept in touch, and when Kennedy was assassinated three years later, Lombardi joined a group of celebrities demanding stricter gun control laws.

In the Kennedy years, Lombardi and football were part of Camelot.

In the Nixon years, the words of football's greatest spokesman and the game itself had become an anathema—in many circles, something to be cursed.

In 1971, Bernie Parrish, a former cornerback with the Cleveland Browns for eight seasons, published *They Call It a Game*, a vicious attack on the NFL hierarchy that called for team owners to be removed and for commissioner Pete Rozelle to be fired. It was a national best seller. Parrish, who was a trailblazer in the National Football League Players Association, said everybody was in on the conspiracy: the television networks, for glamorizing the game; sportswriters, for ignoring the injustices; and Congress, for allowing the NFL to exist as America's only lawful monopoly.

"The con men who sell the National Football League like cosmetics cannot dismiss me as a liar or a hippie or a frustrated marginal player," Parrish wrote. He made claims that his book would lead to antitrust action by Congress and federal probes of the links between the league and the mob. Neither happened. But that's not the point. What Parrish, Meggyesy, and others brought to the surface was not much different from what Harry Edwards preached at the '68 Olympics, or Abbie Hoffman brought to the streets. Football was, again, explaining America.

To explain the connection, look at Hunter S. Thompson, the self-styled chronicler of the counterculture press who created something he called Gonzo Journalism. Writing a piece called

"Fear and Loathing at the Super Bowl" for *Rolling Stone* magazine, Thompson explained his decision to write about Super Bowl VIII as a way of reconciling "the twisted nature of my relationship with God, Nixon and the National Football League."

Super Bowl VIII was played in Miami on January 13, 1974 (the Dolphins beat the Vikings 24–7). Just eight months later, Nixon would resign from the White House in the midst of the Watergate scandal. Thompson was in the midst of his worst phase of drug-addled journalism. He would later say that during the early 1970s he was on the phone with bookies in Las Vegas every Sunday, betting not only each game on the NFL schedule, but sometimes "every down"—wagering how many yards a team would make, play by play, as he watched the game at home on television. So here was the narrative of a football game rewritten with the most decadent intentions by a man who admitted that his passion for the NFL was matched only by the man about to get thrown out of the White House.

Many years later, Thompson was interviewed for a retrospective of the game by NFL Films producer Phil Tuckett. In a long, rambling Q&A, Thompson talked about the summer in the late 1970s he spent around the Oakland Raiders and how he took a liking to the team's mysterious owner from Brooklyn, Al Davis. Thompson said that Davis would ask him about two subjects: Richard Nixon and Adolf Hitler.

"I find often that, most often in fact, that I can transcend what would appear to be huge differences, almost irreconcilable differences between me and somebody else—like George Bush"—with football, said Thompson. "I could probably have a pretty creative and friendly conversation with George Bush. I'm not pitching for that. I wouldn't mind it and he wouldn't either. It's the same thing with Al Davis and Richard Nixon. Extreme freaks recognize each other. Me and Al Davis and Nixon—these are warped people who are good at what they do. Al and I had the same frequency. He got off on Hitler and football, and wow, I was right with him."

That interview took place in March 2003. Less than two years later, Thompson shot himself.

———

In just two decades, the mythology of the game had been packaged for national television consumption, ridiculed as a cause of society's ills, and hijacked by a generation of politicians, new journalists, and broadcasters, all looking for ways to make football work for them.

There was only one way for the game to be, in a word, deloused, and that was to try to sell it the way it had always been sold—through the story of the game itself, the narrative on the field contemplated and executed each week by coaches and players who could be made into big national celebrities.

Put simply, the way to save it was to do what happens on any level of American society. Movies, cars, sports—doesn't matter. Sell it on a grand scale.

Make it into a big show.

———

Postscript: In March 2008, Brett Favre made it official: he announced he was retiring from pro football—making his last pass an interception, making him the only quarterback in NFL history to throw a pick in overtime in two postseason games.

Favre's retirement was broadcast live on ESPN.

9

*"It ain't no mystery
If it's politics or history
The thing you gotta know is
Everything is showbiz."*

—from the Broadway show *The Producers*

How Football Explains
Show Business

The look on Bill Belichick's face always seems to be saying the same thing: I'm just a football coach. Fame is an irritant, an embarrassment. I'm here, in front of these cameras, talking to you people—the mob of reporters with Dunkin' Donuts on their breath and skepticism in their hearts—because I have to be.

But not this morning. This morning, January 29, 2008—five days before Super Bowl XLII—Bill Belichick looks like he might want to play along. It's Media Day, that strange custom where no less than 4,000 credentialed members of the Fourth Estate—from Montreal to Manhattan to Mexico City—are invited by the people who run pro football to mingle among the players and coaches of each team, ask questions, take notes, and cobble together some kind of coherent report to disseminate to their readers and viewers, or just launch into the living, breathing stratosphere of information known as the Internet. Headline from this snapshot: Belichick Smiles.

Why wouldn't he be smiling? In five days, the New England Patriots—the team Belichick has personally crafted year by year,

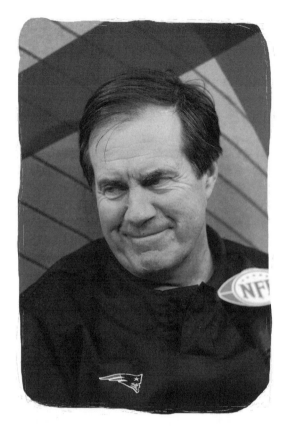

Patriots head coach Bill Belichick cracks a smile during the three-ring circus known as Media Day just days before Super Bowl XLII.

day by day for eight seasons—will attempt to become the first in NFL history to finish with 19 wins and no losses. And, after the first 18 wins, Belichick had refused to, well, play along—not with history, or the media's expectations of it. He had refused to be part of the weekly hype machine promoting the Patriots' perfection on television, refused to indulge the questions about his place in the record books. Week after week, he had kept his foot down, pushing his players to achieve a perfect record, but his lips sealed about his intentions or his motivation. The message: there will be no celebration of history until history is, in fact, made. Yet, after each win, linebacker Tedy Bruschi would be the one to put the team together in the locker room and—before the reporters and their cameras and notebooks were allowed in—would lead the team in a chant called "Aw, yeah!" And after beating New York to finish the regular season undefeated, the "Aw, yeahs!" sounded like wild ghosts howling in the basement catacombs of Giants Stadium. It was the way the players released what Belichick held inside.

What he held inside he learned from his father, Steve Belichick, who coached at the Naval Academy through the terms of eight American presidents. He coached young men who would go on to fight in five wars and many who would enjoy the glory of pro football, including one who would win the Heisman Trophy.

Roger Staubach, the quarterback who would become Navy's all-time greatest player and win a Super Bowl with Tom Landry in Dallas, remembers that Steve Belichick always had his son around to help with the team chores, sometimes staying on the field long after others were gone, fully dedicated to the idea that he would someday be a football coach. "He was always like a mascot," said Staubach. "He was always there." There was no getting around it: young Bill, an only child, was his father's son—gruff, single-minded, and hardened by his Croatian heritage in working-class eastern Ohio.

There was a story—two parts legend, two parts fact—that in October 1962, when President John F. Kennedy went on national television to warn the Soviet Union about stationing nuclear missiles in Cuba, Steve Belichick wasn't too happy about the distraction. Once the president's address was over, the members of the Navy team looked around at each other, wondering about their fate. "Oh my goodness, we're talking about World War III here," said Tom Lynch, a retired navy officer who played linebacker and center at Annapolis from 1961 to 1963. When the lights were turned back up, Belichick said it was time to return to the projection room to get the scouting report for the game the following week against the University of Pittsburgh. "He had smoke coming out of his ears, 'Don't these people know we have Pitt this week?'" said Lynch. It might have been an attempt at diffusing the tension in the room, or just another example of Belichick's unparalleled focus. Either way, the story illustrates that he was a football coach, first and foremost—and his son would be, too.

And during this run to perfection for the New England Patriots more than 45 years later, that devotion was beginning to take its toll. Even Tom Brady—the celebrity golden child of pro football—acknowledged what many of the players had been feeling: "We've been under so much pressure from the coaching staff around here." It was a chilling remark that came one week before departing for the Super Bowl, and hardly anyone cared to notice.

So, it was a tad abnormal to see Belichick achieve a smile five days before the big game. Maybe it was because nobody was asking him about Spygate. Maybe it was because he was simply swept away by the pageantry of Media Day. Maybe it was just the question: he was asked to help a reporter reveal "the inner Bill Belichick," and was told that a number of players have been asked the same thing.

So he smiled, and said, "I'll bet that's been entertaining."

———

Of course, Belichick's words were delivered with a healthy helping of sarcasm. He might have been only joking, but for the past 50 years the National Football League has been dead serious about making its game more and more a grand set piece of American entertainment, a genuine element of one of the country's greatest contributions to world culture: show business.

Football as showbiz was a natural. Walter Camp figured that out in 1891. That's why the rules were changed to create a clear story line, to invent the position of quarterback as individual protagonist—it had all the makings of compelling dramatic action. With the rules changes, the violence of man against himself and the field—already a compelling imitation of life in America itself—took on another, easily defined dimension, yard by yard. It was live theater, with real blood, real winners, and real losers in a finite time period on a field laid out before the audience like the territory of the country itself.

When television came along in the mid-1950s, football already had a very dedicated following. First there were the Ivy League teams, then Notre Dame in the '20s and '30s, and Army in the '40s, and Michigan and California and, eventually, Alabama and a growing number of rivals down south. So, the national audience was there, it just needed to be introduced to the game on a massive scale—like *I Love Lucy* and Milton Berle.

Bert Bell, who preceded Pete Rozelle as commissioner, doesn't get enough credit for signing the first television contract with CBS in 1956. The NFL did grow dramatically as a result of that TV exposure. But CBS profited immensely, driving more Americans to their entertainment programming. The football games were just something to put on the tube on Sunday afternoons—something that had its own story line to sell other stories.

But you could hear Lucy and Desi and Fred and Ethel. On Sunday afternoons, you could not hear the football drama, only the announcers interpreting the events. So, the CBS News division decided that there had to be some way to get the viewer closer to the action, get them inside the story. Isn't that the dream that most of us have—to see how we do on stage, or in front of the microphone? The performer is always acting out our greatest fantasy—to be the guy hitting the home run, the girl in the musical lead, the guy making that one play that ignites the crowd on Sunday afternoon.

On November 30, 1959, Sam Huff—the middle linebacker of the New York Giants—was put on the cover of *Time* magazine. He was Red Grange, Glenn Davis, or Doc Blanchard—or any one of those college football greats—but with something they never had: uniquely powerful entities like *Time* and CBS right in his backyard. In Huff, the world's media capital had the perfect national symbol to redefine how the game was presented, how the story was told.

It was the CBS News division, developing ideas for its new show called *The Twentieth Century*, that came up with a unique gimmick—something that would reinvent storytelling on a football field like nothing else in sports. Huff was mic'd up.

In the 4-3 defense, there are three linebackers—the WILL, or weak-side linebacker; the SAM, or strong-side linebacker, which usually lines up over the tight end; and, the MIKE, the middle linebacker. How ironic that the MIKE linebacker would be the first football player mic'd up. CBS News put a microphone in Huff's helmet, and on the evening of October 30, 1960, in black-and-white on America's TV sets, the game of football came alive.

It was called "The Violent World of Sam Huff," and it was narrated by America's most venerated newsman, Walter Cronkite. Here are Cronkite's opening remarks: "If you were a middle linebacker for the New York Giants. And your name was Sam Huff. This is what it would be like." With those words, Cronkite was trying to put the home viewer, the member of the audience, on stage—in this case into the game of football itself. And as Cronkite finished those words, the camera panned from him to a screen with Huff, wearing No. 70, in action on the field. He had a transmitter attached to his back, an antenna down his leg, and a microphone snapped to the breast plate of his shoulder pads. He snorted, huffed, and shouted, before delivering his body to the ball carrier. "You're going to be closer to pro football than you've ever done before," Cronkite promised.

And then to make no mistake about what CBS was selling, Cronkite made it clear that the days of college football on center stage were over—America, he said, used to worship "Saturday's hero," but now Huff and his teammates were "Sunday's idols."

Many years later, Huff said he understood exactly what was happening at the time. "We were entertainers," he said. "I thought it brought people into the game that had never been into the game before." Once, while Huff was mic'd up, another player hit him with a cheap shot. Huff could be heard threatening to hit him if it happened again. But afterward the offender told Huff he was just trying to get on TV.

Critics hailed "The Violent World of Sam Huff" as groundbreaking television. One from *Time* magazine wrote that it was like being "on a battlefield." Huff played along with the war metaphor, saying to Cronkite, "we have an expression...either kill or be killed."

Being the most violent sport, football has always lent itself to these kinds of hyperbolic characterizations. But now television indulged and, in fact, promoted it. Still, this was only the beginning. Being a news broadcast, the CBS program on Huff was presented in the bare bones. The only sound was Huff's voice and the collisions on the field. There were a few grunts or groans from other players. But there were no barking coaches. No crowd noise.

And no music. It was like a studio technician had laid down the structure of a song on a single track. The next step would be for the musicians and the producer to provide the other tracks with the harmonies and vocals. For football, that producer turned out to be a guy who had been selling overcoats for his father-in-law's clothing company in Philadelphia.

Two years after CBS aired its news special on Sam Huff, NFL commissioner Pete Rozelle got lucky. Like any entity that is looking for ways to ensure that its achievements are preserved for posterity, the NFL had started to sell the filmmaking rights to the championship game, which—up to then—had really been nothing more than highlight reels that resembled the old *Victory at Sea* movies shown to kids between matinees on Saturday afternoons during World War II. Then along came Ed Sabol. Born in Atlantic City in 1909—before the forward pass was commonly used—Sabol had a love of sports. He was a champion swimmer in high school at Ohio State. After getting out of college, he got married and one of his wedding gifts was a 16mm Bell & Howell camera. With the birth of his son, Steve, Sabol did what a lot of fathers did those days—he began his movie-making career. Steve getting his first haircut. Steve's first pony ride. Steve's first football game. This was the extent of Ed Sabol's filmmaking experience when he bid for the right to make the NFL Championship Game film in 1962.

Rozelle, in a foreshadowing of what would happen with the television networks two years later, put the rights out to bid. Ed Sabol's bid was $5,000—double the 1961 price. But Rozelle remained skeptical. After all, other than filming his son, Sabol had no experience. But Sabol—remember, he made money selling overcoats for his father-in-law—sold Rozelle on a bold plan: he would double the number of cameras to eight and use slow motion and other techniques to bring the fan closer to the action.

The 1962 NFL Championship Game was at Yankee Stadium. The Green Bay Packers at the New York Giants. It was December 30 and it was so cold that Sabol's cameras nearly seized up in the icy winds. Vince Lombardi's Packers—used to playing in those conditions—held off the Giants for the second straight year, winning 16–7.

Several weeks later, Rozelle invited the New York press to Toots Shor's—New York's premier bar and restaurant for celebrities, athletes, writers, and the city's business elite—for the debut of Sabol's first film. It was called *Pro Football's Longest Day*—an unabashed reference to *The Longest Day*, the smash hit Hollywood epic about D-Day.

Starring some of the world's greatest actors, including Henry Fonda, Sean Connery, Richard Burton, and, of course, John Wayne—America's leading man who had portrayed football players, frontiersmen, cowboys, and soldiers in countless films—*The Longest Day* was really the first film to mix the often glorified storytelling of World War II with some of the more gruesome details of the greatest amphibious assault in the history of warfare, the Normandy invasion in June 1944. It was more than three hours long and nominated for six Academy Awards, winning three. It was released in the summer of 1962, six months before the Packers played the Giants in the championship game.

Watching Sabol's film, it's easy to see why he borrowed from that title. Using dramatic narration from Chris Schenkel, slow-motion action, and zoom lenses, Sabol focused in on the faces and the movements of the players and coaches, particularly Lombardi, who looked like George S. Patton, demonstrative and demanding, moving his players like troops on a battlefield. (Of course, the Patton image is a bit of license. "Old Blood and Guts" was not involved in the D-Day invasion, except as a decoy.)

Rozelle loved Sabol's film. Who wouldn't? Sabol had taken a sporting event and created a piece of art. Up to that point, with a few exceptions, football movies had been filled with sentimental soppiness or slapstick comedy, with the game on the field being reduced to occasional feats of phony masculinity—the exact antithesis of what it meant to the players, coaches, and, most important, the fans.

Sabol took the naturally complex and compelling narrative of the game itself, which had already mesmerized generations of Americans, and dressed it up with music and ground-breaking filmmaking techniques, some of which were rarely in use even in Hollywood at the time. And, most important, Sabol's film was a natural progression from what CBS presented in its feature about Huff: the football player as the Sunday afternoon warrior. That did two things. Like CBS, Sabol had again suggested the real action was not happening on Saturday afternoons, the domain of college football. And he honed his lens on the one central characteristic of football that had been captivating from the beginning: the brutal violence of the sport.

With one stroke of inspiration, Sabol had amped up football's showbiz appeal.

Sociologists would rail against this glorification of violence, calling Sabol's work propaganda for the NFL. But Rozelle recognized what he had. And in the spring of 1965, Sabol's company was bought by the league and renamed NFL Films. That fall, Sabol's first big project was called the *NFL Game of the Week*. It aired on CBS.

———

Television now needed football more than ever. For 10 years, CBS had learned to appreciate the storytelling power of the game. Now with these new storytelling techniques, it was the perfect storm—a sport that more than anything mirrored the country's reliance on physical struggle, instant gratification, and a win-at-all-costs attitude happening right in your living room each Sunday afternoon. It was like going to worship at the altar of the national zeitgeist right after coming home from church.

In his book *They Call It a Game*, Bernie Parrish summed up the private thoughts of many NFL players who saw the new national marketing trends and techniques as an intrusion, a toxic infiltration of their private domain—and most important as something they had very little chance of benefiting from. Chapter 8 of his book is called, appropriately enough, "Show Biz Arrives." "By 1965," Parrish wrote, "our dressing rooms were aflood with show-biz types. Long hair, dark glasses, large gold cufflinks and dress shirt with ruffles down the front, accompanied 'fabulous sweetie,' and 'beautiful baby, set the camera up over here' into the sanctuary of our locker rooms." Forty years later, it's the players with the designer sunglasses and the bling on their cufflinks. But that would take years and years of labor struggle and free agency, which would not come until 22 years after Parrish wrote his book.

In the meantime, Rozelle, the former Los Angeles ad man who had spent his previous life learning how to make TV executives happy, put the league's broadcast rights out to open bid for the first time in 1964. NBC bid's was $20.6 million for two seasons. ABC came in at $26.4 million. The CBS bid doubled its previous contract of $14.1 million per season, coming in at a total of $28.2 million. CBS knew that football was the ideal lead-in programming for its new magazine news program, *60 Minutes*. So, the network's bid included a bold proposition: a Sunday doubleheader. It was a dynamic formula for building CBS into America's premier television network—for news, entertainment, and sports, and pro football was at the core.

NBC lost the battle, but not the war. The American Football League, then broadcast by ABC, immediately contacted NBC executives who wanted into the football storytelling business very badly. (This can't be stressed enough: TV needed football, just like *The Philadelphia Inquirer* sold newspapers with the Miniature Gridiron in the late 1890s). NBC proposed to double ABC's deal to about $7.5 million per season—still half what Rozelle got out of CBS. But Rozelle was raising all boats. The power of the NFL made the AFL flush with cash—through show business.

The players started to cash in by pitting the two leagues against one another—Joe Namath being the most famous example, signing a $427,000 contract with the New York Jets, the AFL team owned by David Abraham Werblin, the chairman of the Music Corporation of America. His nickname was "Sonny, as in Money," and he knew a few things about how to make money telling stories in America. Werblin's company had created the popular NBC program *Wagon Train*, the nation's top-rated show in the early 1960s. America still feasted on stories about the pioneers. And Werblin saw the story-telling potential of football in the same light. He bought the Jets, and signed Namath—just like he signed every big star in the MCA stable of talent (Liberace and Dean Martin, among others).

"He was the best salesman in the television industry, without question," said agent Al Rush, who helped Werblin sell *Wagon Train* to NBC.

By 1964, watching football on television had become so popular that CBS bid $28.2 million for a two-year contract with the NFL.

In Werblin, Rozelle had met his match. The only way to stop the war was to join forces. The negotiated settlement, the merger of the NFL and the AFL, took more than 18 months to finish. In the meantime, there had to be a big show—everybody agreed on that. It would happen in Rozelle's hometown of Los Angeles: a showdown between the AFL champions, the Kansas City Chiefs, and the NFL champions, the Packers of Vince Lombardi.

Lamar Hunt, the owner of the Kansas City Chiefs, proposed calling this big game "The Super Bowl," after watching his children playing with the Wham-O sensation at the time, called a "Super Ball." Rozelle thought it would never fly. But network television executives knew it when they saw it—that's what it was: the TV executives dubbed the AFL-NFL World Championship Game on January 15, 1967, "Super Sunday." So, what the pro football impresarios thought was too hokey, the TV networks defined, packaged, and sold. Every story needs a title.

Here's the showbiz book on Rozelle: when he took office as the NFL commissioner in 1960, Rozelle presided over a 13-team league playing a 12-game schedule. On many Sunday afternoons, many stadiums were half empty. And the American television audience was being introduced to a new way of telling its old football stories. In the span of just 10 years, the size of the audience exploded. When the Kansas City Chiefs beat the Minnesota Vikings 23–7 in Super Bowl IV in New Orleans on January 11, 1970, 60 million Americans watched the game on television, a bigger TV audience than watched Neil Armstrong take "one small step for man, one giant leap for mankind" six months earlier.

By 1975, there were 26 teams playing a 14-game schedule. And two years later, a Louis Harris poll found that 70 percent of the nation's sports fans said they followed pro football. Only 54 percent cared as much about Major League Baseball, the poll found.

But in the grand tradition of Walter Camp and George Halas and Paul Brown, Rozelle and the NFL kept thinking about ways to grow their sport, expand their influence, especially in the intensely competitive world of popular culture. Blockbuster movies such as *Star Wars* and *Jaws* changed the way entertainment executives approached storytelling. Bigger was now definitely better. And the NFL was certainly not going to get left behind.

Can't Touch This

On the surface, the new NFL was becoming wildly popular. But a closer look revealed that defense was dominating the game. In the early 1970s, Don Shula's "No-Name Defense" reigned supreme. For the remainder of the decade, the "Steel Curtain" of Pittsburgh Steelers defensive coordinator Bud Carson, coaching under Chuck Noll (who played for Paul Brown in Cleveland in the '50s) established a dynasty that rivaled the Packers of the '60s. And while the Super Bowl grew into a bigger and bigger event, the game itself was becoming more and more controlled by superior defensive players who were allowed to get away with pretty much anything. From the seasons of 1969 to 1977, only four of the nine Super Bowl losers scored 10 or more points; in fact, six of the nine losers failed to reach double digits. For four straight Super Bowls—from the seasons of 1971 to 1974—the losers were held to a touchdown or less: Miami, Washington, Minnesota, and Minnesota again.

Before the 1977 season, the NFL owners, meeting in the swanky Biltmore Hotel in Phoenix, Arizona, adopted sweeping changes designed to ban certain defensive tactics that had been allowed to evolve unchecked over the years. First to go: the head slap. It was invented by pro football's first real horror show, defensive end Deacon Jones, who played for the Los Angeles Rams and invented the term quarterback "sack." Jones would take his padded right forearm and—thwap!—smack the helmet ear hole of offensive linemen, often knocking them senseless. Three years after Jones retired, his terrorizing tactic was outlawed.

Next to go: hitting the wide receivers all the way through their pass routes down the field. The new rule stated the receivers could only be hit once. But the impact was not immediate. In the 1977 season, the average points scored per NFL game was 34.4, which means each team was scoring about 17.2 points a game, reaching the end zone no more than twice in a 60-minute contest.

So, in the spring of 1978, the league adopted two more changes designed to enhance the passing game—in other words, get scoring up. First new rule: wide receivers cannot be touched five yards beyond the line of scrimmage. Second: in pass blocking only, offensive linemen could extend their arms and open their hands. The pendulum had swung from the Deacon's head slap to protecting the quarterback at all costs. Can't have showbiz without a show. And the passing game was the NFL's show.

The following year, Edward DeBartolo Jr., who had recently purchased the San Francisco 49ers, hired Bill Walsh as his new head coach. Walsh wasted no time introducing the so-called West Coast offense, which effectively replaced the running game with short passes—perfectly suited for the league's new emphasis on scoring. Walsh drafted a skinny kid with plenty of moxie and more than enough arm to run this new offense—Joe Montana of Notre Dame. Walsh was the architect and Montana the ringmaster of the NFL's new show. The 49ers, who had won exactly nothing since being birthed into the old All-America Football Conference in 1946, rattled off four of the next nine Super Bowl championships.

In 1981—the season of the Niners' first championship—scoring was up across the league. The average points scored in a game jumped to 41.4—up a full touchdown in just four years. With Cool Joe at the helm, Bill Walsh was called "the Genius."

In the early '80s, it was all West Coast, all the time. The Oakland Raiders won the 1980 championship. The Niners won the following year. Two years later, the Raiders, now playing in Los Angeles, won again—and San Francisco the following year. California show time had arrived in the NFL. And in the White House was a former California governor, Ronald Reagan. By using a bunch of pitchmen who brought an unprecedented level of scripted show business to Washington, the old Gipper won two terms. The Reagan presidency itself was showbiz as statecraft. Howard Baker and Roger Ailes wrote the script and Reagan read the lines and took the cues. It all culminated in the 1984 reelection ad campaign that used the slogan, "It's morning in America again," which was written by a little-known ad man named Hal Riney—from San Francisco.

New Kids on the Block

The story of the rise of the San Francisco 49ers was told by a little-known television reporter on a fledgling cable network. His name was Chris Berman. And the network was the nation's first 24-hour sports station: ESPN, which brought an unprecedented level of show business to the idea of selling sports to America around the clock. Berman, a graduate of Brown University who has near total recall, was on the field when Dwight Clark hauled in Joe Montana's perfect pass to beat the Dallas Cowboys in the 1981 NFC Championship Game—"The Catch" passed the NFL torch from America's Team to the high-flying Niners of Bill Walsh.

And the NFL found a new storytelling partner in a whole new television medium, not to mention another pot of gold.

(Full disclosure: I have worked for ESPN, covering the NFL, since 1995. And just in case you're wondering, I'm not going to write anything negative about my company. First of all, I don't have anything negative to say. Second, this is not that kind of book.)

Here are the facts: in 1987, the chairman of the league's broadcast committee at the time, Art Modell, the former owner of the Cleveland Browns before they moved to Baltimore in 1995, announced that the NFL had granted the first cable rights to ESPN, which was already carrying the NFL Draft and the *NFL Game of the Week*, produced by NFL Films.

In 1985, six years after it launched, ESPN showed its first profit, about $1 million. A year later, with the help of the first subscriber fees in the cable business, that profit jumped to almost $40 million. That made ESPN a player, and it bid for the rights to televise NFL games on Sunday nights. For the next 18 years, ESPN *Sunday Night Football* was the highest-rated show on cable television. But the association with football did more than merely fill a prime viewing slot. It allowed ESPN to expand in a way never seen before in the cable industry, adding five new channels, a radio network, a magazine, and the most popular sports-related internet site in the country. (We'll get back to that in a moment.) ESPN, worth close to $30 billion in 2007, makes up nearly half the worth of the global Disney empire.

Its core audience—18–34-year-old males—gave ESPN the power to regenerate the NFL's following, which in the early 1990s was being threatened by Michael Jordan and the NBA on television, as well as the increased participation of young people in the game of soccer. In many suburbs, the "soccer moms"—meaning mostly white middle- and upper-class women—did not want their young boys playing football at an early age. Soccer became an alternative. Violence out, plenty of exercise in. Hundreds of thousands of young boys play soccer in every suburb in America—some of them year-round on travel teams. Some of them go off to play in college. Most do not. Either way, when they grow up, most of them are not watching soccer on TV—David Beckham or no David Beckham.

Why? It helped that pro football had new storytelling partners. Chris Berman had the charm and schtick. Dan Patrick and Keith Olbermann were irreverent. *SportsCenter* had the breaking news, and it was always on. But while ESPN spread the word of the game from coast to coast, new NFL commissioner Paul Tagliabue, who took over for Rozelle in 1989, still envisioned future encroachment into pro football's hold on the show business of sports. He needed a new showbiz guy, somebody who could provide the rocket fuel for the new millennium. That guy was Rupert Murdoch, the dynamic Australian press baron who had bought Fox Television in Los Angeles.

In 1993, with Air Jordan beginning his unparalleled rise to the top of the international sports world, the NFL's television contract was expiring and Tagliabue was looking to make a big statement. Murdoch made it for him. Murdoch needed the NFL. He was trying to build a fourth TV network to challenge CBS, ABC, and NBC. Murdoch offered the NFL a whopping $4.38 billion deal—double what the owners were getting. And just like that, CBS—the network that put the NFL on the map, put a microphone on Sam Huff, and put the showbiz into the football's storytelling tradition—was out.

Murdoch took the CBS broadcasting team of Pat Summerall and John Madden and, with the power of his Los Angeles–based operation, marketed the league to a younger, hipper audience that was attracted to the newest face on TV: Bart Simpson. He was an irreverent smart aleck—just like Bugs Bunny was for the fathers of the kids watching *The Simpsons*—who would be bigger than Fred Flintstone and George Jetson combined. And Fox, which had no sports department when Murdoch made his NFL bid, used the storytelling power of pro football to grow into a meganetwork with some of the country's most-watched programming, including the runaway hit *American Idol*, a modern-day version of *The Gong Show* which spawned an endless number of imitators throughout the television industry—*The Biggest Loser, Dancing with the Stars*, and on and on. It was showbiz writ large, because the studio audience and the audience at home became part of the show, calling in their votes, deciding who gets the gong.

Playing along, feeling like you are part of the show, or part of the story—that's what those CBS News producers were thinking when they mic'd up Sam Huff: how to get the audience closer to the action. Fox just saw the future, and delivered.

Television created a "triumph of expertise," said Michael Oriard, the Oregon State professor who played for the Chiefs in the early 1970s. By getting the fans closer and closer to the game, they felt part of the story. The result was the fan was given the right to feel like an integral part of the action. Do that, Oriard says, and you build blind brand loyalty to your sport. "From a sport not even sportswriters could follow, football has become a game about which every fan can feel expert," said Oriard.

The next logical step was something that had been invented by a couple of football freaks who called themselves the Greater Oakland Professional Pigskin Prognosticators League.

Fantasy Football

Finding your fantasy. No doubt if you are reading this book, you are in a fantasy football league or know someone who is. About 18 million people played fantasy football in 2007. That's more than double the number who played fantasy baseball—even though each baseball team plays a 162-game schedule over a 25-week season, and each NFL team plays 16 games over a 17-week schedule. Fantasy football is a multibillion-dollar industry that—after pornography— is the number two reason why people log on to the Internet.

What fantasy football does is put the storytelling of the game into the hands of the spectators. It is the ultimate in audience participation—but way beyond that. In fantasy football, the audience actually gets to tell its own story, blurring the lines between the competitor and the spectator that not even a visionary like Walter Camp could have predicted.

"It makes the fan feel connected to the game and the players in ways they never were before," said Matthew Berry, the senior director for fantasy sports at ESPN. Berry knows something about storytelling—spending years trying to make it in the unforgiving world of Hollywood screenwriting. At ESPN's headquarters, he oversees a growing empire where millions of football fans get to write their own fantasy about their own pro football team and players every season.

For the longest time, the NFL kept fantasy football at arm's length. The thinking: that fantasy play was dumbing down the game's appeal and legacy. That all changed in 2003 when an industry study found that fantasy football players watch three hours more football per week than the average fan. As any TV executive will tell you, "time spent viewing" is the mother's milk of the advertising dollar.

Another study found that fantasy was not just a safe haven for geeks and shut-ins. Just the opposite. The average fantasy football player is a marketer's fantasy: 36 years old, college educated, married with kids, and an annual income of $75,000. "These are the guys buying flat-screen TVs, trucks, and beer," said Berry. "Just what advertisers are looking for."

A brief history: in the late 1950s, a man named Wilfred Winkenbach, who would later become a limited partner in the Oakland Raiders in the old AFL, started something called fantasy golf. There would be a draft, and each member of the league would pick a team of professional golfers, and at the end of a tournament the team with the lowest combined score would win the pot. It was a way to legally gamble on golf. Baseball was next. Soon, Winkenbach turned to football, a game with an endless number of ways to use numbers to compete and gamble. (Remember, Hunter S. Thompson would bet the number of yards gained on each down.)

Fantasy football now can be played on your TV, your laptop, your mobile device, and your phone. It has launched a multimillion-dollar industry of DVDs, TV shows, magazines, and websites for drafts, teams, leagues, and statistical updates.

And all of it comes down to one simple concept: it's a way to make the audience feel part of the story, part of the show. It is a direct descendant of the "Miniature Gridirons" in front of *The Philadelphia Inquirer* building in the 1890s—the first real attempt to take the story off the page and make it come to life away from the field. Instead of the fans walking or taking a horse and buggy to the newspaper building, now a DSL cable brings it to them in a matter of seconds.

In football, the story was always there. Show business—whether it's on TV or the Internet—just made it much more accessible, and thus very, very big.

———

And Super Bowl XLII between the undefeated New England Patriots and the unappreciated New York Giants turned out to be the biggest show of them all.

This show was supposed to be a coronation. But everything that happened in the final 48 hours leading up to the kickoff suggested otherwise. Two days before the game, U.S. Senator Arlen Specter of Pennsylvania, the ranking Republican on the Judiciary Committee, questioned why Commissioner Roger Goodell destroyed the tapes and notes he confiscated from Bill Belichick and the New England Patriots back in September. Then, the day before the game, the *Boston Herald*, using a single unnamed source, reported that the Patriots had videotaped the walk-through of the St. Louis Rams the night before Super Bowl XXXVI in the Super Dome in New Orleans in 2002. The Patriots issued a curt statement denying it happened.

The *Herald* story was not true. The Patriots did not tape the Rams walk-through. In May 2008, the *Herald* apologized for their mistake. But the damage was done. The night before the Super Bowl, Goodell dispatched two of his lawyers to the Patriots' hotel to question three members of the Patriots staff about the *Herald's* allegations, disrupting the team's preparations and angering Belichick.

Before the game on Super Sunday, February 3, 2008, Belichick was near the Patriots bench, chatting with team owner Robert Kraft and his wife, Myra. Goodell came over to greet them. He shook Kraft's hand and pecked Myra on the cheek. Belichick walked away, barely acknowledging the commissioner.

When the two teams were announced to the University of Phoenix Stadium crowd, the Giants roared onto the field, whooping and hollering like a pack of wild dogs. The Patriots nonchalantly jogged toward their bench with very little fanfare or energy.

Trey Wingo, my colleague at ESPN sitting next to me in the auxiliary press box, turned to me and said, "They look flat."

And outcoached. For some reason—Belichick never stayed around long enough after the game to explain it—the Patriots never did much to adjust to the Giants' blitz package. In the end, Tom Brady—the quarterback who had always prided himself on knowing where "they" were coming from—spent most of the day ducking out of the way of pass rushers: the ageless Michael Strahan, the marvelous Osi Umenyiora, the relentless Justin Tuck. Brady was sacked five times—more than any other postseason game of his career—and hit another 23 times. He was constantly on his back, and the Patriots did very little to give his offensive line—three-fifths of which was headed to the Pro Bowl—much help.

Still, it was Brady and the Patriots. And so, with 2:39 remaining in the fourth quarter, New England held a 14–10 lead. Tedy Bruschi & Co. had held its territory firm, allowing the young apprentice Eli Manning just one trip down the length of the field for a touchdown.

In only one other Super Bowl had the lead changed hands in the final 30 seconds. That was Super Bowl XXIII, when the big showbiz of the 49ers was in full swing, and the great maestro himself, Joe Montana, orchestrated the game-winning drive in the final moments of the fourth quarter to beat the Cincinnati Bengals by four points.

Young Eli couldn't match Montana, could he? Waiting for the answer, most of the country hoped it would be "yes"—that's what most polls showed, at least. America wanted the Patriots dynasty to die, and was riveted to the final act of this drama to see if it would go down.

Eli Manning's final drive to win Super Bowl XLII consisted of 12 plays. Two of them got all the attention—David Tyree's improbably acrobatic 32-yard catch and Plaxico Burress's touchdown grab to win the game. Neither one was as critical as the only run of the drive, which came on the only fourth-down play of the drive.

It was fourth-and-one. The Giants were stuck in their own territory, just 1:28 left. It was do or die. Make the first down, or hand possession of the football back to the Patriots—just like football's founding fathers drew it up in 1880, when the games of soccer and rugby were jettisoned to provide more drama and intrigue.

The Giants' offensive coordinator, Kevin Gilbride, who was once punched on the Houston Oilers sideline by fellow coach Buddy Ryan because he was throwing the ball too much, decided not to pass the football. In from the sideline came the Giants' heavy package, running back Brandon Jacobs and fullback Madison Hedgecock.

"Tedy Bruschi was in the hole," said Hedgecock. "He dove for my legs, tried to chop me. I knew I had to get as low as he was, lower even." Bruschi—who started the 2007 season making a stand against the New York Jets at Giants Stadium—was dug out of the hole by Hedgecock, clearing the way for Jacobs, who fell forward for a two-yard gain. Drive, season, dream preserved.

Less than a minute later, Burress was fancy steppin' in the end zone, and less than two days later, in Manhattan's Canyon of Heroes, Eli Manning, Tom Coughlin, and Michael Strahan would climb onto the back of the same flatbed truck, hoisting the Vince Lombardi Trophy, clearing the confetti from their disbelieving eyes.

Troy Aikman didn't believe it. The former Dallas Cowboys quarterback, a three-time Super Bowl champion, was partnered with play-by-play man Joe Buck, providing his unusually understated but incisive analysis for the Fox TV broadcast team. While it happened and weeks later, Aikman still could not understand how the Patriots allowed history to slip through their fingers. Only six weeks earlier—in a game in Buffalo that the Giants won to clinch a playoff berth—Manning was permitted to throw only one pass in the final quarter of play because the coaches didn't trust him with the football. That same quarterback had conquered the team America had come to love to hate, the empire of Belichick and Brady, and Spygate. "They could very well have been the best football team ever—and had they won the game, that's how they would've been remembered," said Aikman. "It's amazing how one game, one moment in one game, can change perception, can change everything."

We've seen this movie before. Daniel Boone defies the wilderness. Red Grange gallops through bewildered defenders. John Wayne leads his men into celluloid battle. Johnny Unitas prevails in the twilight of a decade and Yankee Stadium. Joe Namath and Luke Skywalker create a sense of everlasting hope. Eli Manning—the protagonist of this story—beats what they're about to anoint as the best team of them all.

"That," said Aikman, "is I guess what makes this game so great."

The story line that had always been there wrote itself across the biggest stage. As Manning's pass landed softly in Burress's white gloves, more than 111 million Americans were watching, the largest for a sporting event in U.S. television history.

"Football brings out the sociologist that lurks in otherwise respectable citizens."

—George F. Will

How Football Explains
Us All

When Eli Manning's pass settled gently in the hands of Plaxico Burress, and the crowd at University of Phoenix Stadium in Glendale, Arizona, finally settled on the idea that the New York Giants were in fact going to beat the New England Patriots, Ray Odierno, the army lieutenant general in command of the multinational forces in Iraq, started yelling like a schoolkid, screaming halfway around the world in his Baghdad office that the team of his childhood had just won the Super Bowl—a nice little distraction for a man who has spent more than 24 months on the front line in America's war on terror.

"It was like we were at the game," he said. Odierno had crammed as many men in his office as he could—nearly four dozen—to watch the Super Bowl. Watching the game, following the story of the season, this is how soldiers keep the pace of their distant lives on schedule with the home front, a way to stay connected—despite the nine-hour time difference. A 1:00 PM Sunday afternoon kickoff at Giants Stadium gets under way at 10:00 PM in Baghdad. Sunday and Monday night games don't start until 4:00 or 5:00 in the morning. "The soldiers get up to watch them religiously to see their team play," he said.

Odierno knows he's lucky to be alive. On the morning of August 21, 2004, a rocket-propelled grenade slammed into the side of his Humvee. He lost his left arm. Three years to the month after surviving that attack, Odierno wrote Tom Coughlin a letter, which the Giants head coach read aloud at the team's annual kick-off luncheon in Manhattan. "You will have a fan here in Iraq and I will be watching whenever I can," Odierno wrote. "Push them hard and remind them, 'team first.'" Odierno's letter got a rousing ovation.

Now, 8,000 miles away, Odierno was cheering, with his men, for a team and a game that somehow was making them all forget the lost lives, the lost limbs, and the lost time in Iraq. Odierno knows the comparisons between war and football are misguided, but he understands how the game explains the American military culture. "To get anything done in the military, you have to work together," he said. "It is not a game of one individual doing it. It is about team. It is about having total dependence on the person to your right, the person to your left, the person behind you, the person in front of you. Football is the same way. It is also about sacrifice and leadership. It is all the same things."

About six weeks after the Super Bowl, Odierno came back to North Jersey. His son Tony was with him. They had a private meeting with Coughlin and took a picture with the Lombardi Trophy.

———

"Football explains America," said Tom Coughlin, "because it is a game in which you have to pay a great price just to have the opportunity to be in a position to compete on game day and have a chance to win. Football is a game in which you are totally dependent on a great many of your teammates in order to have a chance to succeed. You can't succeed in football without your fellow teammates and your fellow teammates have to have the same goal, the same commitment, and the same amount of sacrifice. You find that as you draw parallels from the history of America, for example, World War II. You find that with tremendous sacrifice on the part of individuals comes a great camaraderie and that camaraderie, in many ways, shapes and forms and provides the kind of satisfaction that lasts a lifetime for people who have that experience. Those that don't participate in the game of football or haven't paid that kind of price don't understand what I am talking about. Many people don't achieve the ultimate goal in a game. But those that win their high school championship, win their league title, they still feel a very close association with teammates if those teammates have looked at the competitive opportunity with the same attitude that you have. In other words, if the game is important to you and you take it seriously and you are willing to pay the price, the more of those guys you surround yourself with, the greater the experience and the greater the opportunity to have a bond.

"I was a part of a team that won a high school championship two years in a row and there is a tremendous bond between those guys that I played with even to this day. That is what it means to me when you say that football exemplifies the American way of life. The other aspect of it is the idea of at many times being the underdog and everyone telling you that you don't have a great chance, you don't have a chance to win, and that motivation inspiring you and your teammates to be the very best you can be. When something is accomplished with that kind of challenge put in front of you, it is again, to me, the American way. From the time the immigrants landed on the shore and had the challenge of starting a new life—it parallels that."

———•———

NFL commissioner Roger Goodell: "Football is often called 'America's Game' or 'America's Passion' and there is so much about our game that captures the spirit of our country. When you combine the physical challenges, collective goals, and multiple sacrifices that are required to play football, you are talking about the same values that are at the core of our national spirit. America is about the freedom to compete and be successful on a level playing field. Likewise, football is about teamwork and camaraderie, competition and passion, strategy and energy, strength and emotion. And it's about new challenges and new opportunities every day. I don't think there's much question about it. You can look at football and see the heart of America."

———•———

"How does football explain America? Well, the question is a little lofty for an ink-stained guy like me," said Peter King of *Sports Illustrated* and *Football Night in America* on NBC, "but I believe football tells universal truths in our society. Maybe this story will explain it.

"When my daughter Mary Beth was in middle school, I coached her youth softball team in Montclair, New Jersey. On the schedule coming up on a May evening was a game against Bloomfield, a local power. Bloomfield owned us. In the four or five years I'd been coaching, no team of mine had ever beaten Bloomfield, and the mastery continued up the food chain, too—our high school team rarely beat our neighboring town. Frankly, the kids on our team were a little spooked by Bloomfield and thought they weren't as good. They weren't, but I didn't want them to be beaten before the game started.

"I'd covered Bill Parcells quite a bit in his coaching career, and so I picked up the phone a few days before the game, briefed him on my mission, and asked for his advice.

'What kind of kids do you have?' he said. 'Smart kids? Competitive kids?'

'Real smart,' I said. 'A couple of valedictorian candidates someday.'

'Let me think for a minute here,' Parcells said, and he thought for a bit, and then he came back with, 'You got a scoreboard at the field where you'll be playing?'"

'Yep.'

'I want you to ask the smartest kid on your team to bring her report card in the day you play Bloomfield,' Parcells said. 'It'll probably have all As on it. Then you hold up the report card and tell them, 'You guys are all great in the classroom. Look at this report card—all As. So you do great in school. See that scoreboard over there?' And make sure they all look out at the scoreboard. Tell 'em, 'That scoreboard is your report card out here. You all work hard to be good softball players, the same way you work hard to be good students. There's no reason why you can't have the same success here on this team as you have all day in school.'

"'I love it,' I said. 'I'm going to do that.'

'The thing about motivating your players is the same about motivating my players,' he said. 'Success in football starts with the same thing you use to succeed in anything in life: your head. Just think. That's all—think. There's not a lot about football that's different from other games, or other things you try to make people do. What I try to do is figure out in all players what button I can push to get the best out of them. It's no different than a teacher or a boss or a coach in some other sport.'"

"You're going to want to know the score, of course," King said. "We lost 6–5. I never asked the kids if they liked the speech, or if it meant anything, but I do know this: we lost the game late, and we were not afraid. I've told the story a few times over the years, and people always want it to end with a win for us. Softball's not that way. Neither is football. Neither is life. But I always thought the lesson that day was the win."

———

"How does football explain America? It's the violence of the sport, the violence of the sport attracts us to the game," said Troy Aikman, the former Dallas Cowboys quarterback who won three Super Bowls and now is the game's leading broadcast analyst.

———

The latest immigrant culture to find a home in the game of American football comes from the Polynesian Islands.

"It is because of the way the Polynesian culture is set up—chiefs rule villages," said Vai Sikahema, who was the first NFL football player from the South Pacific island of Tonga. "And they rule islands. Questions weren't asked or posed to the chief, or they were killed. So, the idea of a football coach, the one guy in charge, was always perfectly acceptable to their Polynesian athlete. That father figure on the field works in our culture because it *is* our culture. It's that way in their homes. Fathers have ultimate authority in their homes. That's the nature of our people."

In 2007, there were more than two dozen NFL players of Polynesian descent—from Junior Seau of the Patriots to Haloti Ngata of the Ravens to Ma'ake Kemoeatu of the Panthers to Toniu Fonoti of Atlanta to Troy Polamalu of the Steelers to Lofa Tatupu, who went to three straight Pro Bowls for the Seahawks and recently signed the richest contract for any Polynesian player—six years, $42 million. Tatupu, a deeply religious man, signed the contract two days before Easter Sunday. "It's a great Friday," he said.

The Polynesian islands were changed dramatically in the mid-1800s when Christian missionaries arrived. But not everything changed. The Christian "Mosaic Law" fit right in with Polynesian culture. "In Polynesia, it's an eye for an eye," said Sikahema. "It's not uncommon—even in modern society—for old men to duke it out. I've seen it in my own family. Even at weddings or celebrations, if two people have an issue, they fight. When the fight's over, they gather and they hug and they kiss. But families regularly settle their disputes that way. At its core, it's a warrior culture. That's why football fits in so perfectly."

The influx of Tongan boys into the school system in Euless, Texas—not far from Dallas—has made the local high school football team a spectacular success. The Euless Trojans won the Texas 5A Division 1 championship in 2005 and 2007. Before each game, the Tonga boys lead the team in the Haka—the ancient Polynesian war chant that calls for a fight to the death. The All Blacks rugby team of New Zealand—also consisting of many Polynesian players—has made the Haka their signature pregame ritual. Before the game, the All Blacks will actually face their opponents and do the Haka, finishing with a slash of the throat.

"We're the Italians and Irish of this century—we've only been in this country for 30 or 40 years, so our culture is still very much with us," said Sikahema, who was a record-setting punt returner in the NFL from 1986 to 1993. "Culturally, the fact that 300-pounders can be nimble on their feet, it is because they grew up doing these dances—the Haka. The fire knife dances. The hand-eye coordination that it takes to do these things. The warrior way. It's all why we have become so closely aligned with football as a way to get our way into American culture. It was my ticket here."

Now, it's not unusual for the Sikahema household in suburban Philadelphia to be the host for young Tongan and Samoan athletes who want to make it in American football. "There is no Polynesian word for *cousin*," he said. "We are all brothers. We say *cousin* because it doesn't translate well in America. But the son of my father's brother is not my cousin. He's really my brother. So we all treat each other like that. And it's the same way for any teammate. We are all brothers. Polynesians instantly connected to the American game of football in that way—belief in the father figure structure, warrior culture, and the fight to the end. There is only one way—to fight until you win."

———

"The thing is the abject finality of the game," said sociologist Harry Edwards in explaining how football explains America. "You have 16 games. You have one Super Bowl. You don't get shots at it like in the World Series or the NBA. You don't lose a game on Sunday, and it's, 'Well, what the heck, we're gonna play again on Tuesday or Thursday.' You lose that game on Sunday and it stays with you the whole week. You live with that. That means that everybody has to suck it up and realize that the most important thing that we have to do right now is to win this next game. That kind of intensity brings out relationships, brings out a sense of commitment to each other and the game that you really don't see in other sports.

"The other thing is that when you pay the price that football players pay, you have to really love the game. You can play basketball and not really love and respect the game. You can like to play. You can like to be in the uniform. You can like to be at center stage. But, in football, you're all covered up. Nobody really sees your face. All they know is your number, and that's how they know you're on the field. You're out there taking those hits. You cannot sustain playing if you don't love the game, and the intensity of that feature, of the hits, of the sacrifice, with no guaranteed pay. It's not like in basketball where your salary's guaranteed. Or baseball where your salary's guaranteed. You're one busted knee away from getting a medical settlement, and you're done. But that love of the game is there. When those guys say, 'Hey, man, I really love you and I'm so happy that you're here,' they mean it. I mean they mean it at a level that you don't see in families. They mean it at a level that you only see by guys, from guys who have gone through war together or who will have each other's backs in a police department or fire department. It's that level of intensity."

———

Dallas Cowboys owner Jerry Jones: "Hitting another person is not a natural act, and it hurts. It requires passion, commitment, and determination. It is also a very humbling experience, because on every play it is someone else's job to try to put you on your backside. The game defines the country in so many ways because it captures the essence of one of the fundamental elements of the American spirit. When someone knocks you down, you have to get back up again.

"How we respond to getting knocked down—and the manner in which we get back on our feet—speaks volumes about the character of an individual. As a country, we have been knocked down a few times, but we have always bounced right back up. That resiliency and that determination are what Americans believe in. If you keep sticking your nose in the fight, if you keep working as a team, if you keep your eye on the goal, then good things can happen. Everything that happens in football happens in real life. And everything that happens in real life also happens in football."

———

"When I first started playing football, I didn't realize how being part of a team is so much like being a citizen of the United States—

I do now," said Hall of Fame tight end Ozzie Newsome, general manager and executive vice president of the Baltimore Ravens, the first African American executive to lead his team to a Super Bowl title. "Both are about individuals being part of a larger group with the success of the individual leading to the success of the team and country.

"To succeed in football," said Newsome, "you first have to be accountable to your teammates. That comes from doing the work necessary to achieve on the field. But, even when you do all the right things to become an accomplished player, your success will still depend on the 10 teammates lining up with you. While you're accountable for doing your job, the success of the team is dependent on all 11 doing their jobs.

"So it is with our country. How strong we are as a nation is totally dependent on each of us being accountable to each other. From citizen to citizen, from citizen to leader, and from leader to citizen—our success is based on all of us taking the responsibility to be accountable to one another. There's freedom to succeed in football and with my country. And, in both situations, I have the responsibility to be accountable to my teammates and fellow citizens. When we all take responsibility and follow through with the correct actions, our country is better, just like my football team succeeds when we are accountable to each other. Football success is based on a team winning, and teams win when individual players are accountable to their teammates. Our country's success is raised when we are accountable to each other in our everyday lives."

"This question transports me back to my youth," said Bob Papa, the play-by-play voice of the New York Giants. "There was nothing greater than the anticipation of Christmas morning and the wonderful gifts clustered under the Christmas tree. I get to relive that same sensation as an adult for 17 NFL Sundays: the thrill of a Sunday morning, scouring through a local newspaper while nursing a cup of coffee, while imagining the possibilities of the day on the field. And finally the moment arrives: 1:00 PM. and kickoff. As the action begins I feel like a kid ripping through the wrapping paper of a present. Each NFL game represents a different present for me. I am totally intrigued by the possibilities of each contest.

"The intrigue that surrounds each game can be quite personal. Some love the raw physical attributes of the game. Others prefer the athletic beauty performed on a weekly basis. For me, the greatest aspect about the game is the anatomy of the play. What makes it all work or fail? From the early days of our great nation, Americans have been explorers and adventurers. Those who spread our borders from the eastern seaboard to the west set forth with a plan to stake their own piece of land. Isn't that what each play in football is all about? Securing a portion of real estate? Those early explorers needed to rely on each other to survive the challenges before them. Isn't that what football is all about? It is 11 explorers working together trying to secure their piece of the field. Plotting and planning to achieve their ultimate goal of finding the end zone."

"There is only one way to answer that question of how football explains America and it sounds hokey, but it's true—it's the fans," said Colts quarterback Peyton Manning, the MVP of Super Bowl XLI. "The fans form these allegiances in each city and it creates a level of excitement wherever you go. Fans have an identity with their team and their player and that attachment is something you can feel. It's a sense of belonging—to a team, to a city, to the country, too. Wherever you go, you can feel it each and every Sunday. I think that defines what the game is and how it explains America."

———•———

Lesley Visser, sideline reporter for CBS-TV, and at the *Boston Globe* the first woman to cover an NFL team, the New England Patriots: "When I started covering the NFL in the early 1970s, the credentials said, 'No Women or Children in the Press Box.' It was unheard of for a woman to cover football, and that's because football, war, and Wall Street had always belonged to men. Football was the safe equivalent of battle and money, at the center of our culture. It took women a while, but we now participate in board rooms, on the sidelines, and as secretary of state.

"We are an optimistic country, and we love competition. Football represents hard work, problem-solving, and passion. Americans like to think of themselves as strong and noble. Football players are our gladiators. For women, we're finally on the bus. More women watched the Super Bowl than the Academy Awards last year. I always used to say that men weren't born recognizing a safety blitz, that they loved and learned the game, just like we have. We celebrate football just like our fathers, brothers, uncles, and cousins. My hope is that it gives new meaning to the term *Hail, Mary!*"

———•———

"My father, Walt, loves football, having spent decades as a referee and public address announcer," said Michael Smerconish, conservative commentator on CNN and MSNBC and The Big Talker 1210-AM in Philadelphia. "He likes to explain the significance of football in America by drawing a comparison to our military. Military service begins with basic training, so does football. Before exercises, the military do recon of the enemy while football teams scout their opponents. When the action is over, plays made on the gridiron are evaluated on tape, actions on the battlefield undergo reevaluation. Soldiers are debriefed. Players are dressed down. Relationships established in each extend well beyond the action as participants in each then return to lives among the civilian population. Soldiers and football players take pride in their individual accomplishment all while being a part of a distinctly American team. The result is a combination of strength, power, and camaraderie unrivaled by the armies and athletes of the rest of the world."

Victor Davis Hanson, Hoover Institute fellow at Stanford University: "The values that made America exceptional—the meritocracy, team-work, self-reliance, competition, the desire to win, magnanimity in victory, and resolve in defeat—are on display every Sunday. Players are chosen by their prowess, not their race, tribe, or religion. We want individualists who can improvise, but likewise stress the value of working in unison, not unlike the American military. And of course, we seem to expect that athletes will be extremely well paid, and seek to maximize their market worth, in a way that businessmen, entertainers, and almost everyone else accept. Success on the football field prompts emulation rather than envy. And on the negative side, football is a violent contact sport, unlike soccer, and that too represents much of our frontier past. We are prone to excess and spectacle, like the Romans, and the evolution of football the last 40 years reflects that American trait as well, as we showcase, often crassly so, our national wealth, license, and free expression, from the pregame braggadocio, to the halftime glitz, to the postgame trophies and speeches. Yes, football is American to the core."

The winner of Super Bowl XLI, Tom Coughlin, should have the last thought: "When I was a youngster, we participated in all sports. Quite frankly, it was family, religion, and athletics, and that is the way it was in the little town that I grew up in. That was the reinforcement. All my buddies, their parents felt the same way about it. You got the kind of reinforcement that indicated to you that it was important to be an athlete and it was important to compete and it was important to win.

"When I was very young, Little League baseball was my favorite game, and it was the most recognized of all. As I grew older basketball became a sport that I excelled in. Then by my second or third year in high school, football became the sport that I enjoyed playing the most and that I excelled in. I had an opportunity to gain my college education as a result of that. In high school I began to think that I wanted to be a coach. But when I got to college and played at Syracuse and I played against some of the great college teams in America, it just made me that much more interested in coaching and being a part of something that was very positive and very good in helping individuals, youngsters, be the very best they could be at this particular sport. If some of the values and virtues that could be exchanged could help them in their life, then that would be great, too.

"As a coach, I began at the smallest of levels and eventually the game continued to challenge, and there was success along the way and I advanced career-wise and the game has immersed itself in my lifetime to be an opportunity for me to, again, not only continue to participate against the very best minds in the game of football, but also to raise a family and to educate a family. So what it has meant to me, quite frankly, is that it has been the continuation of the same kind of competitive drive that I had when I was a kid and the opportunities to stay in this for a lifetime and to meet many, many very interesting people, not only in the coaching ranks and the political arena and successful people in business and life, great leaders in the church, and tremendous athletes that I have coached and coached against over the years. It has been for me just a tremendous ride, if you will, or a tremendous opportunity to fulfill an awful lot of dreams and to continue to be challenged literally on a daily basis to be the very best you can be at a very highly competitive sport."

Postscript: In April 2008, Lieutenant General Ray Odierno, the man who helped Coughlin envision a championship, was named commander of all U.S. forces in Iraq.

Acknowledgments

A book like this requires constant support, inspiration, and guidance from a lot of very patient and resourceful people. There are many to thank.

I am especially grateful to the team at Triumph Books, including Mitch Rogatz, Fred Walski, Tom Bast, Paul Petrowsky, and, most of all, Adam Motin, for taking this project and giving it shape.

This book would not have gotten past the title page if not for the help of countless people at NFL Films, the keeper of the keys in the world of football. Steve Sabol gave this book his blessing and kept me thinking. Thank you, Steve.

I am very grateful to NFL Films archivist Chris Willis, whose knowledge of the game is boundless and who has the best football library anywhere. Walter Camp and Parke Davis, who wrote about football more than 100 years ago, are in safe hands with Chris. A special thanks goes to Kathy Davis, Ray Didinger, Bill Driber, Kevin McLoughlin, Ken Rodgers, and Phil Tuckett.

There are some great people at the Pro Football Hall of Fame in Canton, Ohio, who gave countless hours of support and advice.

Joe Horrigan, Ryan Rebholz, and Chris Schilling, thank you for answering all my questions, day and night. Bob Carroll of the Pro Football Researchers Association was an extraordinary help. Thank you, Bob.

I started to think about this book about 15 years ago, when I picked up *Reading Football* by Oregon State University professor Michael Oriard, who played for the Kansas City Chiefs in the early 1970s. Thank you, Professor Oriard, for all your suggestions and help.

Thank you to everybody at the league headquarters, beginning with NFL commissioner Roger Goodell, who has always been accessible and helpful; Joe Browne for his friendship; and Greg Aiello for his fellowship, despite my constant demands.

Time and again I had to reach out to people at many of the 32 NFL teams to check a fact or get research help. So many made themselves available at a moment's notice, but some deserve a special thank-you: Kevin Byrne, Derek Boyko, Pat Hanlon, Patrick Gleason, Dan Edwards, Harvey Greene, Rick Smith, Reggie Roberts, Ted Crews, Paul Kirk, David Tratner, Casey O'Connell, Stacey James, Craig Kelley, Rich Dalrymple, and Dave Lockett.

Thank you to John McDonald and Patrick Carney for their careful editing.

At ESPN I rarely do anything without first consulting Mr. Football Research himself, Russell Baxter. Thank you, Russ, and to every member of the ESPN research staff. And thank you, too, to Vince Doria, Mark Gross, Kathy Kudravi, Mike Leber, Don Skwar, and Norby Williamson for your support.

Many of my friends have helped keep me on track, pushed me along. But none more than Don Sico, whose knowledge of history, politics, and sports were a rare and ready resource. Thank you, Don.

Notes

Introduction

The Steve Mariucci quote is from an NFL Films feature called *Why We Love Football*, 1999.

The Joan Didion quote is from *The White Album* by Joan Didion. New York: Simon & Schuster, 1979, p. 11.

The quote and information about *The Philadelphia Inquirer's* "Miniature Gridiron" are from *Reading Football* by Michael Oriard. University of North Carolina Press, 1993, p. 124–25.

The quote from Oriard on football narrative is from *Reading Football*, p. 85.

The quote from George Lucas is from *Rolling Stone Interviews*, edited by Jann Wenner. New York: Back Bay Books, 2007, p. 147.

The quote from Michael Mandelbaum is from *The Meaning of Sports, Why Americans Watch Baseball, Football, and Basketball and What They See When They Do* by Michael Mandelbaum. New York: Perseus Book Group, 2004, p. 129.

The quote from Franklin Foer is from *How Soccer Explains the World* by Franklin Foer. New York: Harper Perennial, 2004, p. 95.

The Ray Lewis quote is from "The Big Hit," *Sports Illustrated*, July 20, 2007, p. 56.

Chapter One

The quote from Walter Camp is from *American Football* by Walter Camp. New York: Harper & Brothers Publishers, 1891, p. 4.

The quote from Parke H. Davis is from *Football, the American Intercollegiate Game* by Parke H. Davis. New York: Charles Scribner & Sons, 1911, p. 79.

The quote from the *Princetonian* is from *Football, the American Intercollegiate Game*, p. 73.

The quote from Oriard is from an interview on Feb. 19, 2008.

The Forbes quote is from *Reading Football*, p. 229.

Chapter Two

The quotes from Milton Bradley are from "The Meaning of Life" by Jill Lepore in *The New Yorker*, May 21, 2007.

The quote from Camp is from *American Football*, p. 20.

The Oriard quote on Roosevelt is from *Reading Football*, p. 191.

The Davis quote on Roosevelt is from *Football, the American Intercollegiate Game,* p. 111.

The Camp quote about the meeting with Roosevelt is from *Outing,* October 1910.

The Camp quote on personality is from *Walter Camp's Book of Foot-ball* by Walter Camp. New York: The Century Company, 1910, p. 137.

The quote from David Wallace Adams is from *The Real All Americans* by Sally Jenkins. New York: Doubleday, 2007, p. 110.

For a full portrait of Johnny Unitas, read *Johnny U, the Life and Times of John Unitas* by Tom Callahan. New York: Three Rivers Press, 2006.

The Unitas quote is from *The Greatest Game Ever Played* by John Steadman. Stevensville, MD: Press Box Press, 1988, p. 39.

The Accorsi-Davis story and quote is from *The New York Times*, Sunday, Feb. 10, 2008: "The Believer" by John Branch.

Chapter Three

The details of the Gallaudet University football team history come from *The Gallaudet University Football Centennial* by Barry M. Strassler. Washington, D.C.: Gallaudet University Press, 1994.

The Amos Alonzo Stagg quote is from *The Fireside Book of Football*, edited by Jack Newcombe. New York: Simon and Schuster, 1964, p. 244.

The James Webb references and quotes are from *Born Fighting, How the Scots-Irish Shaped America*. New York: Broadway Books, 2004, p. 85.

The quote from Daniel Walker Howe is from *What Hath God Wrought, the Transformation of America, 1815–1848*. Oxford: Oxford University Press, 2007, p. 177.

The quotes from Tocqueville are from *Democracy in America*, edited by J.P. Mayer, a new translation by George Lawrence. New York: Doubleday, 1966, p. 189.

Steve Young quote is from NFL Films feature, *Why We Love Football*, 1999.

Joe Theismann quote is from NFL Films feature, *The Huddle*, 1981.

David Denby quote is from *The Killing Joke* by David Denby in *The New Yorker*, Feb. 25, 2008.

Bill Curry quote is from NFL Films feature, *Why We Love Football*, 1999.

Chapter Four

The quotes from Snoop Dogg are from an NFL Films interview, 2003.

The quotes from Harry Edwards are from an NFL Films interview, 2003.

The story told by Knute Rockne is from *King Football* by Michael Oriard. Chapel Hill: University of North Carolina Press, 2001, p. 294.

The information about the San Jose State–College of Pacific football game program in 1935 is from *King Football,* p. 295.

The quote from Stagg is from *The Fireside Book of Football,* p. 245.

Oriard quotes about early immigrant experiences in football are from *King Football,* p. 260.

W.C. Heinz quote is from "The Ghost of the Gridiron," by W.C. Heinz in *True* magazine, 1958.

The quotes from William C. Rhoden are from author interview, 2008.

The quotes from Charles Ross are from *Third and a Mile* by William C. Rhoden. New York: ESPN Books, 2007, p. 61.

The quote from Tony Dungy is from *Quiet Strength* by Tony Dungy. Carol Stream, IL: Tyndale House Publishers, 2007, p. 49.

Chapter Five

Red Blaik's story about MacArthur at baseball practice is from *American Caesar, Douglas MacArthur 1880–1964* by William Manchester. Boston: Little, Brown and Co., 1978, p. 123.

MacArthur quote about the baseball team celebration is from *American Caesar,* p. 124.

The quote from David Maraniss is from *When Pride Still Mattered* by David Maraniss. New York: Simon & Shuster, 1999, p. 101.

The Lombardi quote about the press is from *Look* magazine, June 1967.

The story from Bill Parcells about Mickey Corcoran is from *No Medals for Trying* by Jerry Izenberg. New York: Macmillan, 1990, p. 33.

Chapter Six

The quote from Harry Edwards is from an NFL Films interview, 2003.

The quotes from Sun Tzu are from *The Art of War* by Sun Tzu, translated by Samuel B. Griffin. London: Oxford University Press, 1963, p. 41.

For the best explanation of how the Battle of Midway was fought and its significance, read *Carnage and Culture* by Victor Davis Hanson. New York: Doubleday, 2001. The quote from van der Vat about Commander Rochefort is from *Carnage and Culture,* p. 372.

The quotes about the new coach-to-quarterback communications are from the minutes of the NFL Competition Committee meeting in the spring of 1994.

Chapter Seven

The story about Coughlin growing up in Waterloo, New York, is from "Giants Seek a Softer Side from Coughlin" by Kevin Manahan in the Newark *Star-Ledger*, June 10, 2007.

The quote from Judy Coughlin is from "Giants Seek a Softer Side from Coughlin," in the *Star-Ledger*, June 10, 2007.

The list of Stagg's inventions in football and baseball is from *The Fireside Book of Football*, p. 244.

The quote from Susan Cheever is from *Prime Times, Writers on Their Favorite TV Shows,* edited by Douglas Bauer. New York: Three Rivers Press, 2004, p. 49 and 51.

The quote from Jack Newcombe about Knute Rockne is from *Knute Rockne, the Man and the Legend,* by Jack Newcombe, in *Sport*, 1953.

The locker room stories about Rockne are from several sources, most notably *The Fireside Book of Football*, p. 266–67.

For a complete history of the rules changes in college football, see *The Anatomy of a Game* by David M. Nelson. Newark: University of Delaware Press, 1994.

The Paul Brown quotes come from *America's Game, The Epic Story of How Pro Football Captured a Nation* by Michael MacCambridge. New York: Random House, 2004, p. 34.

The quotes from Wellington Mara and Tom Landry are from *The Man Inside Landry* by Bob St. John. Dallas: Word Books, 1979, p. 80-81.

The Emlen Tunnell quote is from *The Man Inside Landry*, p. 76.

Chapter Eight

The story about Bart Starr's brother Bubba is from *When Pride Still Mattered*, p. 256.

Vince Lombardi's quote about Starr is from *Run to Daylight* by Vince Lombardi. Englewood Cliffs, NJ: Prentice Hall, 1963, p. 148.

The information about Lombardi's recruiting habits as a high school coach is from *When Pride Still Mattered*, p. 342.

Bart Starr's quotes are from *The Greatest Packers of Them All* by Chuck Johnson. New York: Putnam, 1968, p. 41.

The quotes from Howard Cosell are from *Like It Is* by Howard Cosell. New York: Playboy Press, 1974, p. 18.

For a complete study of American athletics at the end of the 1960s, read Jack Scott's *Athletic Revolution*, New York: Free Press, 1971.

The quote from Edwards is from an NFL Films interview, March 13, 2003.

The quote from Dr. Thomas Tutko is from *Winning Is Everything and Other American Myths* by Thomas Tutko. New York: Macmillan, 1976, p. 19.

The story about the Nixon campaign checking out Lombardi is from *When Pride Still Mattered*, p. 466.

The quotes from Bernie Parrish are from *They Call It a Game* by Bernie Parrish. New York: The Dial Press, 1971, p. xii.

Chapter Nine

The quotes from Tom Lynch are from ESPN, *Sunday NFL Countdown* on Feb. 3, 2008.

The quotes from Sam Huff are from an NFL Films feature called *Linebackers Past and Present,* 2004.

The quote from Parrish is from *They Call It a Game,* p. 122.

The details of the NFL's TV deals in 1964 are from *America's Game,* p. 190.

The quote from Al Rush is from *Namath* by Mark Kriegel. New York: Viking, 2004.

The quote from Michael Oriard is from *King Football* by Michael Oriard. Chapel Hill: University of North Carolina Press, 2001.

The quote from Madison Hedgecock is from "Two Minute Thrill" by Paul Zimmerman in *Sports Illustrated,* Feb. 11, 2008.

The statistics on fantasy sports participation and demographics are from ESPN, the NFL, and the Fantasy Sports Trade Association.

Chapter Ten

The quotes from Ray Odierno are from a Michael Eisen story for the New York Giants website.

The quotes from Harry Edwards are from an NFL Films interview, March 2003.

Author interviews

Troy Aikman, Brian Baldinger, Matthew Berry, Tom Brady, Tedy Bruschi, Plaxico Burress, Tom Coughlin, Tony Dungy, Herm Edwards, Brett Favre, Victor Davis Hanson, Edward Hottle, Jerry Jones, Robin Lester, Ray Lewis, Matt Light, Eli Manning, Archie Manning, Peyton Manning, Ozzie Newsome, Michael

Oriard, Bob Papa, Bill Parcells, Antonio Pierce, William C. Rhoden, Tony Romo, Ed Sabol, Steve Sabol, Jeff Saturday, Vai Sikahema, Michael Smerconish, Stephen A. Smith, Michael Strahan, Amani Toomer, Adam Vinatieri, Lesley Visser, Mike Vrabel, Corey Webster, Jack Whitaker, and Jason Witten. Many others granted interviews but did not want their names used. All were conducted in 2007 and 2008.

Selected Bibliography

Bauer, Douglas. *Prime Times: Writers on Their Favorite TV Shows.* New York: Three Rivers Press, 2004.

Callahan, Tom. *Johnny U: The Life and Times of John Unitas.* New York: Three Rivers Press, 2006.

Camp, Walter. *American Football.* New York: Harper and Brothers Publishers, 1891.

Davis, Parke H. *Football: The American Intercollegiate Game.* New York: Charles Scribner and Sons, 1911.

de Tocqueville, Alexis. *Democracy in America.* Edited by J.P. Mayer. Translated by George Lawrence. New York: Doubleday, 1966.

Dungy, Tony. *Quiet Strength.* Carol Stream, IL: Tyndale House Publishers, 2007.

Foer, Franklin. *How Soccer Explains the World.* New York: Harper Perennial, 2004.

Halberstam, David. *The Education of a Coach.* New York: Hyperion, 2005.

Halberstam, David. *The Fifties.* New York: Villard Books, 1993.

Hanson, Victor Davis. *Carnage and Culture.* New York: Doubleday, 2001.

Hill, Dean. *Football Thru the Years.* New York: Gridiron Publishing Company, 1940.

Howe, Daniel Walker. *What Hath God Wrought: The Transformation of America, 1815–1848.* Oxford: Oxford University Press, 2007.

Izenberg, Jerry. *No Medals for Trying.* New York: Macmillan, 1990.

Johnson, Chuck. *The Greatest Packers of Them All.* New York: Putnam, 1968.

Kriegel, Mark. *Namath.* New York: Viking, 2004.

Lombardi, Vince. *Run to Daylight.* Englewood Cliffs, NJ: Prentice Hall, 1963.

MacCambridge, Michael. *America's Game: The Epic Story of How Pro Football Captured a Nation.* New York: Random House, 2004.

March, Harry. *Pro Football: Its Ups and Downs.* Albany, NY: Lyon Printing Co., 1934.

Manchester, William. *American Caesar: Douglas MacArthur 1880–1964.* Boston: Little, Brown, and Co., 1978.

Mandelbaum, Michael. *The Meaning of Sports: Why Americans Watch Baseball, Football, and Basketball, and What They See When They Do.* New York: Perseus Books Group, 2004.

Maraniss, David. *When Pride Still Mattered.* New York: Simon and Shuster, 1999.

Newcombe, Jack. *The Fireside Book of Football.* New York: Simon and Schuster, 1964.

O'Brien, Michael. *Vince: A Personal Biography of Vince Lombardi.* New York: William Morrow, 1987.

Oriard, Michael. *King Football.* Chapel Hill: University of North Carolina Press, 2001.

Oriard, Michael. *Reading Football.* Chapel Hill: University of North Carolina Press, 1993.

Paolantonio, Sal, with Reuben Frank. *The Paolantonio Report: The Most Overrated and Underrated Players, Teams, Coaches, and Moments in NFL History.* Chicago: Triumph Books, 2007.

Parcells, Bill, with Jeff Coplon. *Finding a Way to Win.* New York: Doubleday, 1995.

Parrish, Bernie. *They Call It a Game.* New York: The Dial Press, 1971.

Piascik, Andy. *The Best Show in Football: The 1946–1955 Cleveland Browns, Pro Football's Greatest Dynasty.* New York: Taylor Trade Publishing, 2007.

Rhoden, William C. *Third and a Mile: The Trials and Triumphs of the Black Quarterback.* New York: ESPN Books, 2007.

St. John, Bob. *The Man Inside Landry.* Dallas: Word Books, 1979.

Scott, Jack. *The Athletic Revolution.* New York: The Free Press, 1971.

Smith, Melvin I. *Early American and Canadian Football: Beginnings through 1883–84.* Self-published, 2003.

Smith, Red. *Press Box: Red Smith's Favorite Sports Stories.* New York: Avon Books, 1976.

Steadman, John. *The Greatest Game Ever Played.* Stevensville, MD: Press Box Press, 1988.

Tzu, Sun. *The Art of War.* Translated by Samuel B. Griffin. London: Oxford University Press, 1963.

Webb, James. *Born Fighting: How the Scots-Irish Shaped America.* New York: Broadway Books, 2004.